Pointers in C

A Hands on Approach

Naveen Toppo
Hrishikesh Dewan

Apress

Pointers in C: A Hands on Approach

ISBN-13 (pbk): 978-1-4302-5911-4

ISBN-13 (electronic): 978-1-4302-5912-1

President and Publisher: Paul Manning
Lead Editor: Saswata Mishra
Technical Reviewer: William Murray, Chris Pappas
Editorial Board: Steve Anglin, Mark Beckner, Ewan Buckingham, Gary Cornell, Louise Corrigan,
    James DeWolf, Jonathan Gennick, Jonathan Hassell, Robert Hutchinson, Michelle Lowman, James Markham,
    Matthew Moodie, Jeff Olson, Jeffrey Pepper, Douglas Pundick, Ben Renow-Clarke, Dominic Shakeshaft,
    Gwenan Spearing, Matt Wade, Saswata Mishra, Steve Weiss
Coordinating Editor: Anamika Panchoo
Copy Editor: Mary Behr
Compositor: SPi Global
Indexer: SPi Global
Artist: SPi Global
Cover Designer: Anna Ishchenko

Distributed to the book trade worldwide by Springer Science+Business Media New York, 233 Spring Street, 6th Floor, New York, NY 10013. Phone 1-800-SPRINGER, fax (201) 348-4505, e-mail orders-ny@springer-sbm.com, or visit www.springeronline.com. Apress Media, LLC is a California LLC and the sole member (owner) is Springer Science + Business Media Finance Inc (SSBM Finance Inc). SSBM Finance Inc is a Delaware corporation.

For information on translations, please e-mail rights@apress.com, or visit www.apress.com.

Apress and friends of ED books may be purchased in bulk for academic, corporate, or promotional use. eBook versions and licenses are also available for most titles. For more information, reference our Special Bulk Sales–eBook Licensing web page at www.apress.com/bulk-sales.

Any source code or other supplementary materials referenced by the author in this text is available to readers at www.apress.com/9781430257882. For detailed information about how to locate your book's source code, go to www.apress.com/source-code/.

To my beloved parents Clement and Xaveria and my dear wife Rashmi

—Naveen Toppo

In memory of my best friend "Neon"

—Hrishikesh Dewan

Contents at a Glance

Contents

About the Authors

Naveen Toppo is currently working as a consultant at the CT DC TEC Division of Siemens Technology and Services Pvt. Ltd India. With a total of over 7 years of experience, his current focus area is in optimum utilization of hardware features (performance engineering).

He is also involved in the research of distributed algorithms used for spatial databases. Prior to joining Siemens, he was technical lead for embedded systems at Wipro Technologies, where he was working on a project on SoC network processors, dealing with L3 layer's routing algorithms.

In his prior roles, he was associated with projects on Intel tablets based on Android platform, development of T9 dictionary support, and parsing and lexical analysis. He has a master's degree in technology in computer sciences from the Indian Institute of Technology Guwahati.

Hrishikesh Dewan has worked as lead engineer for Siemens Technology and Services(STS), INDIA since June, 2008. He is also a PhD scholar at the Department of Computer Science and Automation, IISC, Bangalore pursuing research in the areas of large scale distributed storage systems. In STS, he leads the distributed systems laboratory. Prior to joining STS, he founded a very small open source software development organization named "Srishti" that promoted open source tools and software for schools and colleges. He also worked as a project manager for 2 years at Eth Ltd., a subsidiary and R&D unit of Dishnet Wireless Ltd (Aircel). He is the author of two other books on WCF-SOAP and Visual Studio technologies.

Acknowledgments

I am greatly indebted to my beloved parents Clement and Xaveria and my lovely wife Rashmi, my brother John, and my other brother Kartik for their continuous support and endless patience. I would like to acknowledge my colleague Krishna M.R. for his valuable inputs on the code snippets. I would like to thank all my friends, colleagues and my organization Siemens. Thanks also to all my birding friends. At last, I would like to thank Saswata, Jeffrey, Anamika, and technical reviewers and also all other people from Apress who helped in turning this dream into reality.

Last but not the least, I would like to thank my avian friend "Tickell's blue flycatcher" and all other beautiful birds out there who kept me fresh and motivated to complete the work.

—Naveen Toppo

I am in debt to all the staff of Apress who helped us in preparing the content in a readable format. Special thanks to Saswata and Jeff for providing the opportunity to write this book.

—Hrishikesh Dewan

Introduction

Ever since the introduction of the C programming language in 1978, it has been regarded as a powerful language and has gained popularity among programmers worldwide. Despite starting as a language for the UNIX operating system, it has been used extensively in implementing wonderful and very complex software on multiple platforms. C has always been the default choice of language for writing any low level layers, device drivers, embedded system programming, programming mobile devices and so on.

One of most important features of C is *pointers*, which is an interesting topic and many times difficult to grasp. C being a relatively low level language, requires that programmers are well versed with many fundamental notions of computers while using it. And also, C is not a strongly-typed language.

The concept of pointer is known for its cryptic nature and that makes the understanding of it in some cases very difficult. This book is meant to provide an understanding of the concept of pointers for a novice or an intermediate or an expert programmer. To make the reader understand any concept of pointers we have provided back ground information which is not related to the language but which is part of the computer science literature. This background information will help the reader to understand the concepts very easily.

The book is organized as follows.

Chapter 1 is the basis for other chapters. It describes the concept of memory and runtime memory which provides the reader with an understanding of the basic concept of how memory is accessed and how data/instructions are stored in memory. This chapter helps in understanding the compilation steps. This includes explanation of how intermediate results such as preprocessing, assembly and object code are generated. It also gives detailed background of how memory segments/sections are created by the compiler. Memory segments are explained in detail with pros and cons which will help readers to understand the usage of various kinds of variables. This chapter is also augmented with the understanding of the concept of virtual memory.

Chapter 2 introduces the concept of a pointer variable and the most important operations on it (referencing and dereferencing). This chapter explains the concept of initialization, comparison and memory allocation to pointer variables. It also explains the notion of a NULL pointer, dangling pointer, VOID pointer and CONST qualifiers. This chapter also explains the notion of how a pointer variable is used with different types of primitive data types such as integer, char and so on. This chapter also provides an explanation of how multilevel pointers can be used to access memory addresses and the values stored at those locations.

Chapter 3 contains a detailed explanation of pointer arithmetic and single dimensional arrays. Pointer arithmetic is explained in detailed. Explanation is given on how pointers can be used to access various contiguous memory locations using addition and subtraction operations on pointers. A section in this chapter explains the usage of pointers to access array data types. This chapter gives illustrious insight on how various kinds of expressions can be used to access a particular index of an array.

Chapter 4 contains an explanation of how pointers can be used to initialize static strings and manipulate them. Many examples have been included in the form of basic string manipulation functions such as strcpy, substring and so on. String manipulation is one of the most important requirements while solving and implementing algorithms.

Chapter 5 describes the usage of pointers to access multidimensional memory access, specifically 2-d and 3-d arrays.

Chapter 6 is about the detailed description of how structures and its member fields can be accessed with pointers. Usage of structures and pointers helps in implementing complex and dynamic data structures. Illustrious examples have been included in the chapter to explain the implementation of data structures such as linked lists and binary trees with the help of pointers. A section is also dedicated to explain how a function of a program can be accessed dynamically with the help of function pointers.

Chapter 7 is an explanation of usage of the function pointers concept.

Chapter 8 contains details about file handling. How file pointers are used to manipulate files using write and read system calls have been explained in depth.

■ ■ ■

CHAPTER 1

Memory, Runtime Memory Organization, and Virtual Memory

I have always wondered why the concept of a pointer is so dauntingly difficult to grasp. The concept of a pointer can be intuitively understood only if you are able to visualize it in your mind. By "visualizing" I mean being able to represent mentally its storage, lifespan, value, and so forth. Before getting into the nitty-gritty of pointers, however, you need to be equipped with the concepts of memory, runtime memory organization of the program, virtual memory, the execution model, and something of the assembly language.

This chapter introduces these prerequisite concepts by way of a generic case of how the modeling of runtime organization is done and some simple examples of how a CPU accesses the different sections of a process during runtime. Finally, it introduces the concept of virtual memory.

Subsequent chapters will go through the basics of pointers, their usage, advanced topics of pointer manipulation, and algorithms for manipulating memory addresses and values. The final chapters focus on practical applications.

The chapters are designed to be discrete and sequential, so you may skip any sections you are already familiar with.

Memory and Classification

Memory by definition is used to store sequences of instructions and data. Memory is classified to be permanent or temporary depending on its type. Throughout this work, references to memory are to be implicitly understood as meaning temporary/non-persistent storage (such as RAM, cache, registers, etc.), unless explicitly identified as permanent storage. Memory is formed as a group of units in which information is stored in binary form. The size of the group depends on the underlying hardware or architecture and its number varies (1, 2, 4, 8, 16, 32, 64, or 128 bit).

Classification

Memory classification is the best way to gauge and assess the various kinds of memory available (Figure 1-1).

Type	Capacity	Speed (apprx)	Volatile/Nonvolatile	Cost
Registers	16/32/64 bits, depending on the type of CPU	< 10ns	Volatile	
Cache	in K bytes	10-50ns	Volatile	Increasing
RAM (Main Memory)	in Mbytes; some GBs	50-100ns	Volatile	
Secondary Storage	in GBs and TBs	10 millisec	Nonvolatile	

Figure 1-1. *Memory hierarchy*

Let's take a look at each of these different kinds of memory with respect to their usage and connectivity. Some of the memory could be present inside the chip (on-chip) along with processors, and some are attached to the ports on the motherboard. Communication or transfer of data takes place with the help of the address bus.

- **Registers**: These registers are mainly on the chip along with the processor. Depending on the architecture they vary in numbers. The descriptions below about registers are based on the Intel IA32 architecture.

- **Segment Registers**: CS, DS, ES, etc. These registers help in implementing support for segmentation and eventually to support multiprogrammed environments.

- **System Registers**: CR0, CR1, EFLAGS etc. These registers help in initializing and controlling system operations. Similarly, there are many other registers along with the ones mentioned above. I will not go into detail about each of the other registers.

- **Caches**: Typically, cache is high-speed memory that is used to store small portions of data temporarily. And probably this is the data that will be accessed frequently in the near future. In modern systems, caches also have some hierarchical structure.

  - L1 cache is faster and closer to the CPU but smaller in size.

  - L2 cache is less fast and less close to the CPU but comparatively bigger in size.

  - SRAM is used for cache memories as they are faster than DRAM. Also, there exist dedicated instruction cache and data cache in some architectures, such that instruction code will reside in the instruction cache while the data portion on which these instructions work will reside in the data cache.

- **Main Memory**: In some literature the main memory is also called the physical memory. This is the place where all the data and instruction to be executed is loaded. When a program is executed, the operating system creates a process on its behalf in the main memory. I do not explain this process and its creation in this chapter, but I will do so in detail in subsequent chapters. The capacity of the main memory dictates the size of the software a system can handle. The size of the main memory runs in GBs. Also, the operating system shares part of the main memory along with other processes.

Now that you have a sense of the different kinds of memory in the system and what they do and contain, let's see how they look when laid out and interconnected. Figure 1-2 schematically depicts a typical computer architecture and associated connectivity.

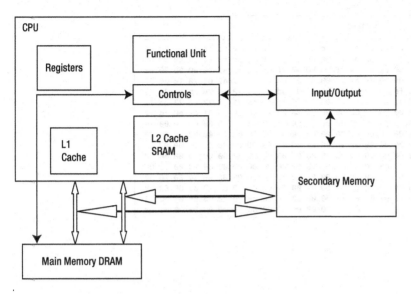

Figure 1-2. *Memory hierarchy layout*

Memory Layout

Memory is a linear array of locations, where each location has an address that is used to store the data at those locations. Figure 1-3 illustrates typical connectivity between the CPU and main memory.

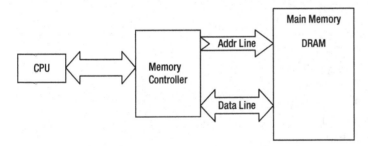

Figure 1-3. *Memory layout*

To reiterate, a memory address is a number that is used to access the basic units of information. By `information` I mean data. Figure 1-4 illustrates a memory dump; in it you can see how data is stored at consecutive locations in memory.

Memory Address	Data
0x0042F6DF	cc cc cc cc cc cc cc cc cc cc cc cc cc cc cc cc cc cc cc cc cc cc cc cc
0x0042F70B	12 cc cc cc cc cc cc cc cc 32 00 00 00 cc cc cc cc cc cc cc cc 14 00 00 00
0x0042F737	00 bf 19 2b 01 01 00 00 00 d8 34 2f 00 b0 48 2f 00 c4 fb 81 50 00 00 00 00
0x0042F763	00 00 00 43 00 00 00 00 00 48 f7 42 00 25 01 00 00 c8 f7 42 00 73 10 2b 01
0x0042F78F	00 9a 33 d8 75 00 e0 fd 7e d8 f7 42 00 f2 9e ad 77 00 e0 fd 7e 2b 11 34 69
0x0042F7BB	00 00 00 00 00 a4 f7 42 00 00 00 00 00 ff ff ff ff d5 71 b1 77 c3 23 da 1e
0x0042F7E7	7e 00 00 00 00 00 00 00 00 00 00 00 00 00 00 00 00 6e 10 2b 01 00 e0 fd 7e
0x0042F813	00 00 00 00 00 00 00 00 00 00 00 00 00 00 00 00 00 00 00 00 00 00 00 00 00
0x0042F83F	00 00 00 00 00 00 00 00 00 00 00 00 00 00 00 00 00 00 00 00 00 00 00 00 00
0x0042F86B	00 00 00 00 00 00 00 00 00 00 00 00 00 00 00 00 00 00 00 00 00 00 00 00 00
0x0042F897	00 00 00 00 00 00 00 00 00 00 00 00 00 00 00 00 00 00 00 00 00 00 00 00 00
0x0042F8C3	00 00 00 00 00 00 00 00 00 00 00 00 00 00 00 00 00 00 00 00 00 00 00 00 00
0x0042F8EF	00 00 00 00 00 00 00 00 00 00 00 00 00 00 00 00 00 00 00 00 00 00 00 00 00
0x0042F91B	00 00 00 00 00 00 00 00 00 00 00 00 00 00 00 00 00 00 00 00 00 00 00 00 00
0x0042F947	00 00 00 00 00 00 00 00 00 00 00 00 00 00 00 00 00 00 00 00 00 00 00 00 00
0x0042F973	00 00 00 00 00 00 00 00 00 00 00 00 00 00 00 00 00 00 00 00 00 00 00 00 00

Figure 1-4. *Memory Dump*

Data and Instruction

Data and instruction are inherent parts of any program. Instructions or program logic manipulate the data associated with the program (Figure 1-5). To execute any program, first the program is loaded with the help of a loader into memory, and the loaded program called a process (an instance of a running program) is loaded by the operating system.

Memory address	Instructions	Data
0041378A	Pop	edi
0041378B	Pop	esi
0041378C	Pop	ebx
0041378D	add	esp,0F0h
00413793	cmp	ebp,esp
00413795	call	@ILT+295(_RTC_CheckEsp) (41112Ch)
0041379A	mov	esp,ebp
0041379C	pop	ebp
0041379D	ret	

Figure 1-5. *Data and instruction*

How the Processor Accesses Main Memory

If we assume that a program is loaded into memory for execution, it is very important to understand how the CPU/ processor brings in all the instructions and data from these different memory hierarchies for execution. The data and instructions are brought into the CPU via the address and data bus. To make this happen, many units (the control unit, the memory controller, etc.) take part.

Let's get into the details of how data is transferred into memory. Assume that the CPU is going to execute an instruction: mov eax, A. This assembly instruction moves the value stored at variable A to register eax. After the CPU decodes this instruction, it puts the address of variable A into the address bus and then this data is checked for whether it is present in the L1 cache. There can only be two cases: if the data is present, it is a hit; if it is not, it is a miss.

In case of a miss, the data is looked for in next level of hierarchy (i.e., L2 cache) and so on. If the data is a hit, the required data is copied to the register (the final destination), and it is also copied to the previous layer of hierarchy.

I will explain the copying of data, but first let's look into the structure of cache memory and specifically into memory lines.

Cache Memory

In generic form, a cache has N lines of addressable (0 - 2N -1) units. Each line is capable of holding a certain amount of data in bytes (K words). In the cache world, each line is called a block. Cache views memory as an array of M blocks, where M = 2N/K, as shown in Figure 1-6. And the total cache size C = M* K.

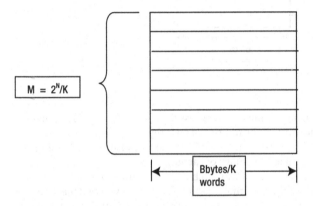

Figure 1-6. *Cache memory model*

Examples of realistic caches follow:

L1 cache = 32 KB and 64 B/line

L2 cache = 256 KB and 64 B/line

L3 cache = 4 MB and 64 B/line

Now you know a little about the structure of the cache, let's analyze the hit and miss cache in two level of caches (L1 and L2). As noted in the discussion of the CPU executing the MOVL command, the CPU looks for the data in the L1 cache and if it is a miss, it looks for it in the L2 cache.

Assuming that the L2 cache has this data and variable A is of 4 bytes, let's see how the copy to the register happens.

Figure 1-7 shows a hit at the L2 cache; the data (4 bytes) is copied into the final destination (i.e., the register eax); and 64 bytes from the same location are copied into the L1 cache. So, now L1 cache also has the value of variable A, plus extra 60 bytes of information. The amount of bytes to be copied from L2 cache to L1 cache is dictated by the size of the cache line in L1 cache. In this example, L1 cache has 64 bytes, so that much data is copied into L1 cache.

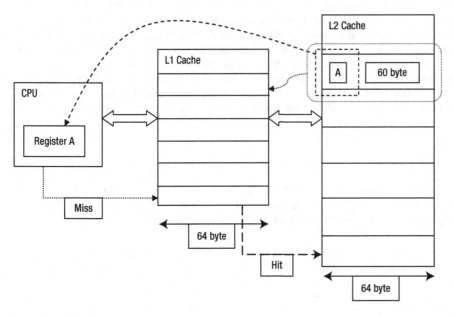

Figure 1-7. *Data fetching scenario*

If variable A happens to be the ith index of some array, that code may try to access the $(i+1)^{th}$ index. This happens when we write a for loop inside which we are trying to iterate over all the indexes of an array.

The next time the CPU accesses the $(i+1)^{th}$ index, it will find the value in the L1 cache, because during loading of the ith index we copied more data. This is how spatial locality takes advantage of caching.

You have seen a case of miss and hit in two levels of cache. This scenario can be extended up to the main memory and beyond to the secondary memory, such as hard disks and other external memory, every time we copy the data back to the earlier level in the hierarchy and also to the destination. But the amount of data copied into an earlier level in the hierarchy varies. In the above case, data got copied as per the size of the cache line; if there is a miss in the main memory, what will copied into the main memory will be of size 1 page (4KB).

Compilation Process Chain

Compilation is a step-by-step process, whereby the output of one stage is fed as the input to another stage. The output of compilation is an executable compiled to run on a specific platform (32-/64-bit machines). These executables have different formats recognized by operating systems. Linux recognizes ELF (Executable and Linker Format); similarly, Windows recognizes PE/COFF (Portable Executable/Common Object File Format). These formats have specific header formats and associated offsets, and there are specific rules to read and understand the headers and corresponding sections.

The compilation process chain is as follows:

Source-code➤Preprocessing➤Compilation➤Assembler➤Object file➤Linker➤Executable

To a compiler, the input is a list of files called source code (.c files and .h files) and the final output is an executable.

The source code below illustrates the compilation process. This is a simple program that will print "hello world" on the console when we execute it after compilation.

Source code Helloworld.c

```c
#include<stdio.h>
int main()
{
        printf("Hello World example\n");
        return 0;
}
```

Preprocessing

Preprocessing is the process of expanding the macros specified in source files. It also facilitates the conditional compilation and inclusion of header files.

In the code snippet in Figure 1-8 for the file Macros.c, the following are the candidates for preprocessing:

- **Inclusion of header files**: util.h, stdafx.h
  When util.h is included, it includes the declaration of the function int multiply (int x, int y).

- **Expansion of macros**: KB, ADD
  These macros are replaced with the actual defined values after preprocessing once the inclusion of the header file is done and the macros are expanded. The output of this phase is passed to the next stage (i.e., compilation).

Original File -------- Macros.c	util.h
```c #include "stdafx.h" #include "util.h" #define KB 1024 #define ADD(v1, v2) (v1 + v2) int _tmain(int argc, _TCHAR* argv[]) { int arr[KB]; int i = 30; int j = 20; int z = ADD(30,20); int k = multiply(30,20); printf("z = %d\n", z); return 0; ```	```c #ifndef _UTIL_ #define _UTIL_ int multiply(int x, int y); #endif ```

Preprocessed File -------- Macros.i

```c
#line 12 "c:\\projects\\pointers\\ptrmemorytest\\stdafx.h"
#line 5 "c:\\projects\\pointers\\ptrmemorytest\\ptrmemorytest.cpp"
#line 1 "c:\\projects\\pointers\\ptrmemorytest\\util.h"
int multiply(int x, int y);
#line 7 "c:\\projects\\pointers\\ptrmemorytest\\util.h"
#line 6 "c:\\projects\\pointers\\ptrmemorytest\\ptrmemorytest.cpp"
int wmain(int argc, _TCHAR* argv[])
{
        int arr[1024];
        int i = 30;
        int j = 20;
        int z = ( 30 + 20 );
        int k = multiply(30,20);
        printf("z = %d\n", z);
        return 0;
}
```

Figure 1-8. Preprocessing step

Compilation

The next process is to compile the preprocessed file into assembly code. I will not go into the details of the compilation process, which itself has several phases such as lexical analysis, syntax analysis, code generation, etc. The output of the compilation process is add.asm/add.s. Below is the listing for the add.c program, which is compiled, and its output can be seen in the listing of file add.asm.

File add.c

```
int add(int v1, int v2)
{
        return v1+v2;
}
int _tmain(int argc, _TCHAR* argv[])
{
        int a = 10;
        int b = 20;
        int z = add(10,20);
        return 0;
}
```

File add.asm

```
;       COMDAT ?add@@YAHHH@Z
_TEXT   SEGMENT
_v1$ = 8                                        ; size = 4
_v2$ = 12                                       ; size = 4
?add@@YAHHH@Z PROC                              ; add, COMDAT
; Line 7
        Push    ebp
        Mov     ebp, esp
        Sub     esp, 192                        ; 000000c0H
        Push    ebx
        Push    esi
        Push    edi
        Lea     edi, DWORD PTR [ebp-192]
        Mov     ecx, 48                         ; 00000030H
        Mov     eax, -858993460                 ; ccccccccH
        rep stosd
; Line 8
        Mov     eax, DWORD PTR _v1$[ebp]
        Add     eax, DWORD PTR _v2$[ebp]
; Line 9
        Pop     edi
        pop     esi
        pop     ebx
        mov     esp, ebp
        pop     ebp
        ret     0
?add@@YAHHH@Z ENDP                              ; add
_TEXT   ENDS
```

```
PUBLIC   _wmain
EXTRN    __RTC_CheckEsp:PROC
; Function compile flags: /Odtp /RTCsu /ZI
;        COMDAT _wmain
_TEXT    SEGMENT
_z$ = -32                                        ; size = 4
_b$ = -20                                        ; size = 4
_a$ = -8                                         ; size = 4
_argc$ = 8                                       ; size = 4
_argv$ = 12                                      ; size = 4
_wmain PROC                                      ; COMDAT
; Line 11
        Push    ebp
        mov     ebp, esp
        sub     esp, 228                         ; 000000e4H
        push    ebx
        push    esi
        push    edi
        lea     edi, DWORD PTR [ebp-228]
        mov     ecx, 57                          ; 00000039H
        mov     eax, -858993460                  ; ccccccccH
        rep stosd
; Line 12
        Mov     DWORD PTR _a$[ebp], 10           ; 0000000aH
; Line 13
        Mov     DWORD PTR _b$[ebp], 20           ; 00000014H
; Line 14
        Push    20                               ; 00000014H
        push    10                               ; 0000000aH
        call    ?add@@YAHHH@Z                    ; add
        add     esp, 8
        mov     DWORD PTR _z$[ebp], eax
; Line 15
        Xor     eax, eax
; Line 16
        Pop     edi
        pop     esi
        pop     ebx
        add     esp, 228                         ; 000000e4H
        cmp     ebp, esp
        call    __RTC_CheckEsp
        mov     esp, ebp
        pop     ebp
        ret     0
_wmain ENDP
_TEXT ENDS
END
```

Assembler

After the compilation process, the assembler is invoked to generate the object code. The assembler is the tool that converts assembly language source code into object code. The assembly code has instruction mnemonics, and the assembler generates the equivalent opcode for these respective mnemonics. Source code may have used external library functions (such as printf(), pow()). The addresses of these external functions are not resolved by the assembler and the address resolution job is left for the next step, linking.

Linking

Linking is the process whereby the linker resolves all the external functions' addresses and outputs an executable in ELF/COFF or any other format that is understood by the OS. The linker basically takes one or more object files, such as the object code of the source file generated by compiler and also the object code of any library function used in the program (such as printf, math functions from a math library, and string functions from a string library) and generates a single executable file.

Importantly, it links the startup routine/STUB that actually calls the program's main routine. The startup routine in the case of Windows is provided by the CRT dll, and in the case of Linux it is provided by glibc (libc-start.c). Figure 1-9 shows what the startup stub looks like.

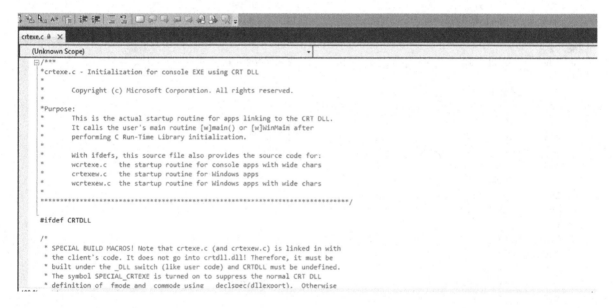

Figure 1-9. *Startup stub*

Figure 1-10 shows a situation where with the help of the debugger the program's main function is being called by another function, _tmainCRTStartup(). This startup routine is the one that is responsible for calling the application's main routine.

```
(Unknown Scope)
                          lpszCommandLine,
                          StartupInfo.dwFlags & STARTF_USESHOWWINDOW
                            ? StartupInfo.wShowWindow
                            : SW_SHOWDEFAULT
                      );
   #else   /* _WINMAIN_ */

   #ifdef WPRFLAG
               __winitenv = envp;
               mainret = wmain(argc, argv, envp);
   #else   /* WPRFLAG */
               __initenv = envp;
               mainret = main(argc, argv, envp);
    #endif   /* WPRFLAG */

    #endif   /* _WINMAIN_ */

               /*
                * Note that if the exe is managed app, we don't really need to
```

```
100 %   ▼ ◄

Call Stack

 Name
 helloworld.exe!add(int v1, int v2)  Line 8
 helloworld.exe!wmain(int argc, wchar_t * * argv)  Line 14 + 0x9 bytes
 helloworld.exe!_tmainCRTStartup()  Line 552 + 0x19 bytes
 helloworld.exe!wmainCRTStartup()  Line 371
 kernel32.dll!7525339a()
 [Frames below may be incorrect and/or missing, no symbols loaded for kernel32.dll]
 ntdll.dll!77289ef2()
 ntdll.dll!77289ec5()

 Call Stack  ▣ Immediate Window
```

Figure 1-10. *Startup stub*

Loader

Strictly speaking, the loader is not part of compilation process. Rather, it is part of the operating system that is responsible for loading executables into the memory. Typically, the major responsibilities of a UNIX loader are the following:

- Validation

- Copying the executable from the disk into main memory

- Setting up the stack

- Setting up registers

- Jumping to the program's entry point (_start)

Figure 1-11 depicts a situation in which the loader is executing in memory and loading a program, helloworld. exe. The following are the steps taken by the OS when a loader tries to load an executable:

1. The loader requests that the operating system create a new process.

2. The operating system then constructs a page table for this new process.

3. It marks the page table with invalid entries.

4. It starts executing the program which generates immediate page fault exception.

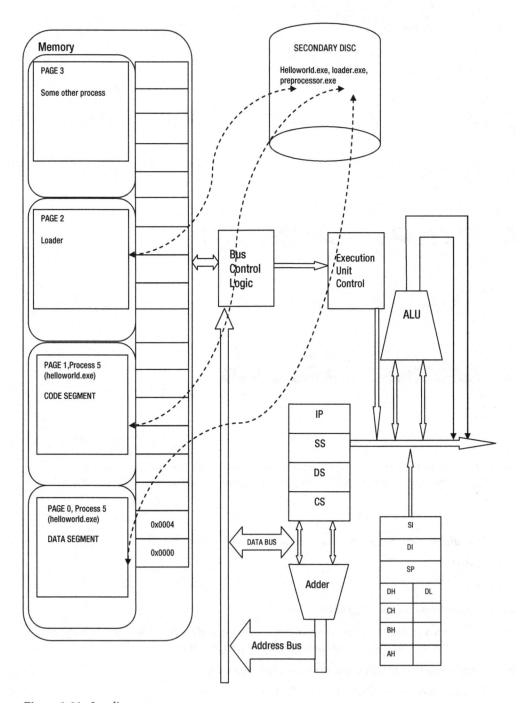

Figure 1-11. *Loading process*

The steps mentioned above are taken care of by the operating system for each program running in the memory. I will not go into the details of the technicalities in these steps; an interested reader can look into operating system-related books for this information.

Let's see how different programs look when they simultaneously share the physical memory. Let's assume the operating system has assigned a process id – 5 for the program helloworld.exe. It has allocated FRAME 0 & 1 and loaded the PAGE 0 & 1 where some portion of code segment and data segment are residing currently. We will look at the details of the different segments depicted in Figure 1-11 later in subsequent sections. Page is a unit of virtual memory and Frame is the unit used in the context of physical memory.

Memory Models

A process accesses the memory using the underlying memory models employed by the hardware architecture. Memory models construct the physical memory's appearance to a process and the way the CPU can access the memory. Intel's architecture is has facilitated the process with three models to access the physical memory, discussed in turn in the following sections:

- Real address mode memory model
- Flat memory model
- Segmented memory model

Real Address Mode Memory Model

The real address mode memory model was used in the Intel 8086 architecture. Intel 8086 was 16 processors, with 16-bit wide data and address buses and an external 20-bit-wide address bus. Owing to the 20-bit-wide address bus, this processor was capable of accessing $0 - (2^{20} - 1) = 1MB$ of memory; but due owing to the 16-bit-wide address bus, this processor was capable of accessing only $[0 - (2^{16} - 1)] = 64KB$ of memory. To cross the 64KB barrier and access the higher address range of 1MB, segmentation was used. The 8086 had four 16-bit segmentation registers. Segmentation is achieved in real mode by shifting 4 bits of a segment register and adding a 16-bit offset to it, which eventually forms a 20-bit physical address. This segmentation scheme was used until the 80386, which had 32-bit-wide registers. This model is still supported to provide compatibility with existing programs written to run on the Intel 8086 processor.

Address Translation in Real Mode

Figure 1-12 depicts how an address translation is done in real mode using segmentation.

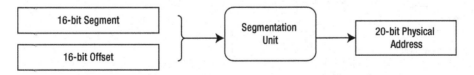

Figure 1-12. *Segmentation in real mode*

Flat Memory Model

In the 386 processor and later, apart from the general-purpose 32-bit registers, the designers have provided the following memory management registers to facilitate more sophisticated and complex management:

- global descriptor table register (GDTR)

- load descriptor table register (LDTR)

- task register

In the flat memory model, the memory space appears continuous to the program. This linear address space (i.e., address space accessible to the processor) contains the code segment, data segment, etc. The logical address generated by the program is used to select an entry in the global descriptor table and adds the offset part of the logical address to the segments base, which eventually is equivalent to the actual physical address. The flat memory model provides for the fastest code execution and simplest system configuration. Its performance is better than the 16-bit real-mode or segmented protected mode.

Segmented Memory Model

Unlike segmentation in real mode, segmentation in the segmented memory model is a mechanism whereby the linear address spaces are divided into small parts called `segments`. Code, data, and stacks are placed in different segments. A process relies on a logical address to access data from any segment. The processor translates the logical address into the linear address and uses the linear address to access the memory. Use of segmented memory helps prevent stack corruption and overwriting of data and instructions by various processes. Well-defined segmentation increases the reliability of the system.

Figure 1-13 gives a pictorial overview of how memory translation takes places and how the addresses are visible to a process.

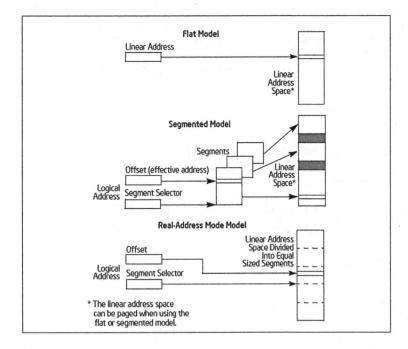

Figure 1-13. Memory models

Memory Layout Using Segments

A multiprogramming environment requires clear segregation of object files into different sections to maintain the multiple processes and physical memory. Physical memory is a limited resource, and with user programs it is also shared with the operating system. To manage the programs executing in memory, they are distributed in different sections and loaded and removed according to the policies implemented in the OS.

To reiterate, when a C program is loaded and executed in memory, it consists of several segments. These segments are created when the program is compiled and an executable is formed. Typically, a programmer or compiler can assign programs/data to different segments. The executable's header contains information about these segments along with their size, length, offset, etc.

Segmentation

Segmentation is a technique used to achieve the following goals:

- Multiprogramming

- Memory protection

- Dynamic relocation

Source code after compilation is segregated into five main sections/segments—CODE, DATA, BSS, STACK, and HEAP—discussed in turn in the following sections.

Code Segment

This segment consists of instruction codes. The code segment is shared among several processes running the same binary. This section usually has read and execute permissions. Statically linked libraries increase the footprints of the executable and eventually the code segment size. They execute faster than dynamically-linked libraries.

Dynamically-linked libraries reduce the footprint of the executable and eventually the code segments' size. They execute more slowly because they spend time in loading the desired library during runtime.

```
Main.c                          foo.c
void main()                     void foo()
{                               {
        foo();                          return;
        return;
}                               }
```

All the generated machine instructions of the above code from Main.c and foo.c will be part of a code segment.

Data Segment

A data segment contains variables that are global and initialized with nonzero values, as well as variables that are statically allocated and initialized with nonzero values. A private copy of the data segment is maintained by each process running the same program.

A static variable can be initialized with a desired values before a program starts, but it occupies memory throughout the execution of the program. The following program illustrates an example where the candidates for data segments are used in the source code.

Source code Main.c

```
static int staticglobal = 1;
int initglobal = 10;
int uninitglobal;
void main()
{
        return;
}
```

The variables `staticglobal` and `initglobal` are part of the data segment.

Uninitialized/BSS Segment

BSS stands for "Block Started by Symbol." It includes all uninitialized global variables as well as uninitialized static local variables declared with the `static` keyword. All the variables in this section are initialized to zero by default. Each process running the same program has its own data segment. The size that BSS will require at runtime is recorded in an object file. BSS does not take up any actual space in an object file. Initialization of this section is done during startup of the process. Any variable that requires initialization during startup of a program can be kept here when that is advantageous. The following source code illustrates an example where the variables declared are part of a BSS segment.

Source code Main.c

```
static int uninitstaticglbl;
int uninitglobal;
void main()
{
        return;
}
```

The variables `uninitstaticglbl` and `uninitglobal` are part of BSS segment.

Stack Segment

The stack segment is used to store local variables, function parameters, and the return address. (A return address is the memory address where a CPU will continue its execution after the return from a function call).

Local variables are declared inside the opening left curly brace of a function body, including the `main()` or other left curly braces that are not defined as static. Thus, the scopes of those variables are limited to the function's body.

The life of a local variable is defined until the execution control is within the respective function body.

```
main.c                        foo.c
void main()                   void foo()
{                             {
int var1;                         int var3;
int var2 = 10;                    int var4;
foo();
}                             }
```

The variables `int var1` and `int var2` will be part of the stack when function `main()` is called. Similarly, `int var3` and `int var4` will be part of the stack when function `foo()` is called.

Heap Segment

The heap area is allocated to each process by the OS when the process is created. Dynamic memory is obtained from the heap. They are obtained with the help of the malloc(), calloc(), and realloc() function calls. Memory from the heap can only be accessed via pointers. Process address space grows and shrinks at runtime as memory gets allocated and deallocated. Memory is given back to the heap using free(). Data structures such as linked lists and trees can be easily implemented using heap memory. Keeping track of heap memory is an overhead. If not utilized properly, it may lead to memory leaks.

Runtime Memory Organization

The runtime memory organization can be viewed In its entirety in the Figure 1-14. You can see that some portions of memory are used by the operating system and rest are used by different processes. The different segments of a single process and different segments belonging to other processes are both present during runtime.

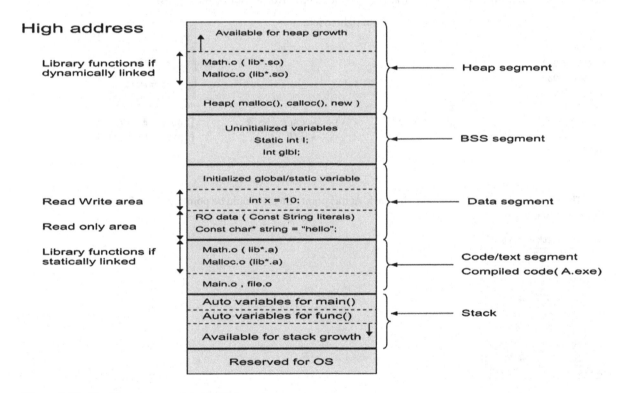

Figure 1-14. Runtime memory organization

Intricacies of a Function Call

When a function call is made, it involves lots of steps that are hidden to the user by the OS. The first thing done by the OS is the allocation of a stack frame/activation record for the respective function call at runtime. When a control returns to the caller after execution of the function, the allocated stack frame is destroyed. In result, we cannot access the local variables of the functions, because the life of the function ends with the destruction of the respective stack frame. Thus the stack frame is used to control the scope of the local variables defined inside a function.

The allocated stack frame is used to store the automatic variables, parameters, and return address. Recursive or nested calls to the same function will create separate stack frames. The size of the stack frame is a limited resource which needs to be considered while programming.

Maintenance of the stack frame and the entities included inside it (local variables, return address, etc.) is achieved with the help of following registers:

- **base pointer/frame pointer (EBP)**: Used to reference local variables and function parameters in the current stack frame.

- **stack pointer (ESP)**: Always points to the last element used on the stack.

- **instruction pointer (EIP)**: Holds the address of the next CPU instruction to be executed, and it is saved onto the stack as part of the CALL instruction.

Steps to Make a Function Call

Let's examine how a function call is made and the various steps involved during the process.

1. Push parameters onto the stack, from right to left.

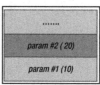

```
0x200000000        main()
0x200000004        {
0x200000084        int x = 10;
0x200000089        int y = 20;
0x200000100        int z;
0x200000104        z = add( 10, 20);     < ------ CALL INSTR
0x200000108        z++;                  < ------ EIP
0x200000110        }
```

Layout of stack at this point

```
[ param #2 (20) ]
[ param #1 (10) ]
```

2. Call the function.

The processor pushes the EIP onto the stack. At this point, the EIP would be pointing to the first byte after the CALL instruction.

Layout of stack at this point

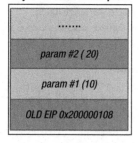

3. Save and update the EBP.

- At this point we are in the new function.

- Save the current EBP (which belongs to the callee function).

- Push the EBP.

- Make the EBP point to the top of the stack:
  mov ebp, esp

EBP can now access the function parameters as follows:

8(%ebp) – To access the 1st parameter.

12(%ebp) – To access the 2nd parameter.

And so on...

The above assembly code is generated by the compiler for each function call in the source code.

Layout of stack at this point

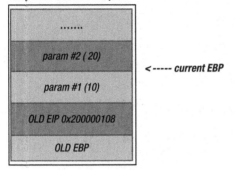

- Save the CPU registers used for temporaries.

- Allocate the local variables.

```
int add( int x, int y)
{
int z;
z = x + y;
return z;
}
```

The local variable is accessed as follows:
-4(%ebp), -8(%ebp) etc..

Layout of stack at this point

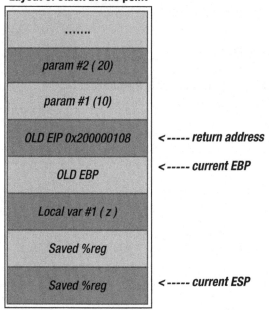

4. Returning from the function call.

•   Release local storage.

•   By using a series of POP instructions

    •   Restore the saved registers

    •   Restore the old base pointer

    •   Return from the function by using the RET instruction

Considering the temporal and spatial locality behavior exhibited by programs while executing, the stack segment is the optimum place to store data, because many programming constructs—such as for loop and do while—tend to reuse the same memory locations. Making a function call is an expensive operation as it involves a time-consuming setup of the stack frame. Inline functions are preferred instead when the function body is small.

Memory Segments

In the previous sections, you saw various segments involved during the runtime of an application. The following source code helps in visualizing and analyzing the formation of these segments during runtime. The program is self-explanatory. It prints the addresses of all the segments and the address of variables residing in their respective segments.

Source code Test.c

```
#include<stdio.h>
#include<malloc.h>
int glb_uninit;  /* Part of BSS Segment -- global uninitialized variable, at runtime it is
initialized to zero */
```

```c
int glb_init = 10;        /* Part of DATA Segment -- global initialized variable */
void  foo(void)
{
static int num = 0;        /* stack frame count */
int autovar;            /* automatic variable/Local variable */
int *ptr_foo = (int*)malloc(sizeof(int));
if (++num == 4)            /* Creating four stack frames */
    return;
printf("Stack frame number %d: address of autovar: %p\n", num, & autovar);
printf("Address of heap allocated inside foo() %p\n",ptr_foo);
foo();                    /* function call */
}
int main()
{
char *p, *b, *nb;
int *ptr_main = (int*)malloc(sizeof(int));
printf("Text Segment:\n");
printf("Address of main: %p\n", main);
printf("Address of afunc: %p\n",foo);
printf("Stack Locations:\n");
foo();
printf("Data Segment:\n");
printf("Address of glb_init: %p\n", & glb_init);
printf("BSS Segment:\n");
printf("Address of glb_uninit: %p\n", & glb_uninit);
printf("Heap Segment:\n");
printf("Address of heap allocated inside main() %p\n",ptr_main);
return 0;
}
```

Output:

```
Text Segment:
Address of main: 00411131
Address of afunc: 004111CC
Stack Locations:
Stack frame number 1: address of autovar: 0012FE5C
Address of heap allocated inside foo() 003A2E78
Stack frame number 2: address of autovar: 0012FD70
Address of heap allocated inside foo() 003A2EB8
Stack frame number 3: address of autovar: 0012FC84
Address of heap allocated inside foo() 003A2EF8
Data Segment:
Address of glb_init: 00417014
BSS Segment:
Address of glb_uninit: 00417160
Heap Segment:
Address of heap allocated inside main() 003A2E38
```

Virtual Memory Organization

Multiprogramming enables many processes to execute concurrently at any given time. It is not necessary that these processes be interrelated. The support is enabled by hardware (the memory management unit) and the operating system. Virtual memory allows the operating system to use system resources optimally. The most important feature of virtual memory organization is the protection of various processes from one another by the operating system.

The features of virtual memory include the following:

- Physical organization

- Logical organization

- Protection

- Relocation

- Sharing

In a multiprogramming environment, many processes share the main memory. A process as a whole sees the main memory as a complete resource dedicated to itself (the process). But the operating system loads/keeps only that portion of a program in memory that is currently required to be executed.

A Glimpse into a Virtual Memory System

Figure 1-15 illustrates how a virtual address space is mapped to a physical address. The main entities that take part in this translation are MMU, TLB, and page tables, described in the next section.

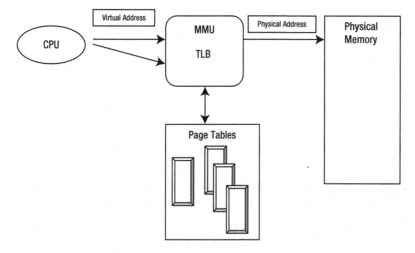

Figure 1-15. *Virtual memory system*

Address Spaces

Memory space has to be shared between two entities:

- The kernel/OS

- The user program

By definition any program, whether an OS or a user program, is termed a `kernel process` or a `user process` when loaded in memory.

Virtual Address Space

Virtual memory is a logical entity whereby a user process assumes that it is loaded. The address pertaining to this virtual memory is called the `virtual address space`.

Figure 1-16 shows a typical scenario whereby a process assumes it is loaded. The virtual address space from 0 - 7FFFFFFE is being used to load the user process. The virtual address 0x7FFFFFFF – higher is used by the kernel. When a program is loaded into memory, the respective process assumes that the whole user space is allocated for the process.

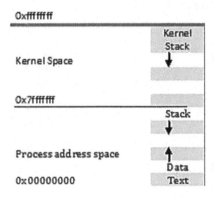

Figure 1-16. *Process's view of virtual address space*

Figure 1-17 shows a typical scenario of how a kernel views virtual memory.

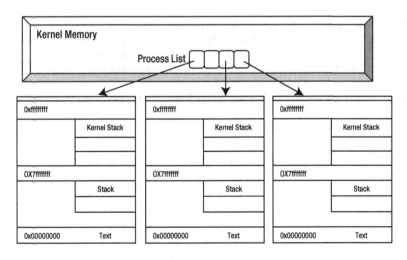

Figure 1-17. *Kernel's view of virtual address space*

A virtual address consists of

- A virtual page number
- A page offset field

Virtual Page Number	Page Offset

31   11   0

Physical Address Space

The physical address space is the actual address in the main memory where the pages are loaded. Figure 1-18 illustrates a typical scenario of how a virtual address is translated into a physical address.

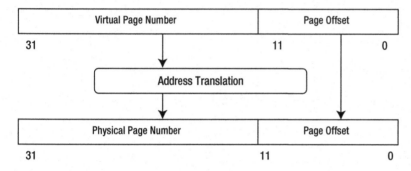

Figure 1-18. *Address translation process*

Paging

Paging is one of the most important parts of virtual memory. This scheme allows the operating system to load and unload the parts of pages of a process to any non-contiguous location of physical memory. The notion of paging assumes that the main/physical memory is divided into equal and fixed size frames/page frames which can accommodate pages of any process. Pages are basically parts of processes that are divided into equal and fixed size, typically 1kb/4kb.

Figure 1-19 illustrates a paging scenario where pages of process A and process B are residing in various frames of physical memory.

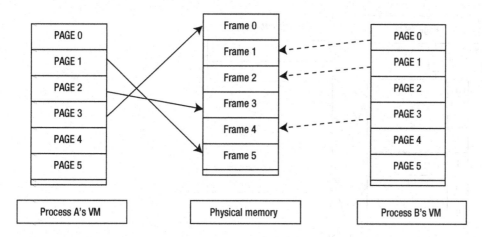

Figure 1-19. *Paging*

The paging system typically addresses the following tasks:

1. **Address Space Management**: Responsible for allocating and managing the address space of processes

2. **Address Translation**: Done by dedicated hardware in the MMU. It also takes care of exception handling (such as page faults)

3. **Memory Sharing:** This is shown in Figure 1-19.

Page Table

The operating system maintains one separate page table for each process executing in memory. Referring to this page table, it deduces whether a valid page is being accessed or some invalid page, in which case it generates a fault exception. Figure 1-20 illustrates a typical page table that is referenced during address translation to get to an actual physical address in memory.

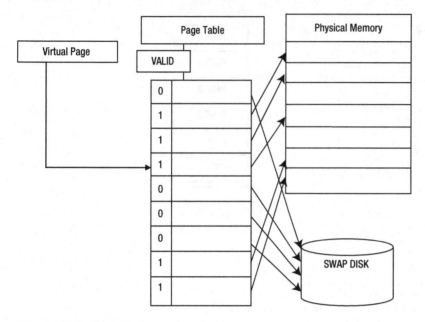

Figure 1-20. *Page table*

Summary

This chapter has discussed relevant aspects of memory—in particular, memory classification and cache memory. Aspects of cache memory that I have not discussed, such as performance optimization and the CPU generating exceptions due to alignment issues, are not required in the current context. The most important section of this chapter is the one on memory layout, which serves to strengthen the knowledge of the reader from a programming as well as from a systems point of view.

The next chapter develops the basics of pointer variable concepts and other details such as memory allocation and its usage.

CHAPTER 2

■ ■ ■

Pointer Basics

Like any other variable, you need to first understand the basics of pointer variables. The basics include declaration, definition, and usage. This chapter explains the concept of pointer variables. The emphasis is on the usage of pointers with the help of diagrams to visualize the concepts. This chapter also explains the inner details of memory allocation and deallocation, and how pointer variables manipulate them.

Pointers by definition are variables used to store memory addresses of data or functions, unlike other data type variables that are used to store only the value. As with any usual variable, a pointer takes space in memory. In the next section, we will concentrate first on the concept of referencing/dereferencing of variables, as it will help visualize how a pointer works.

What is an address of a variable?

Consider the following:

int x = 40;

0x00394768 ----> | x = 40 |

The drawing above shows how a variable *x* of type *integer* is used to store the value of 40. For a program, the variable *x* is nothing but a storage location of some memory address. In the above case, we are storing the value of 40 at location 0x00394768, and this location is referred to by the variable *x*. This also means that any variable we have used in our program refers to some address. If you remember from Chapter 1, there are code segments for each program. The functions also share that part of the memory, and they are loaded at some other part of the code segment itself.

In the above case, we are trying to store an integer value, but notice that a memory address is also a number or value. What if we want to store that number in some other variable? If we want to store or access a memory address (such as 0x00394768) in a variable, we need special variables called pointers.

Address of Operator

You may wonder about the method used to get the address of any variable used in a program. The "address of" operator (&) returns the memory address of the operand. The address of operator is a unary operator, which is applied to variables. The example below shows how the operator gets the address of the variable that is used to store a value.

Source code. Ptr1.c

```
int main()
{
int var_int ;
printf("Insert data\n");
scanf("%d", &var_int);
return 0;
}
```

In the example above, the function scanf uses the "address of" operator (&) to get the address of the variable var_int to store the value entered by the user, because the scanf function should know the address where the value needs to be kept.

Retrieving the Address of a Variable

As mentioned earlier, data is stored in a memory location. The following program illustrates how to obtain the address of the memory location or the address of the variable where data is stored.

Source code. Ptr2.c

```
int main()
{
        int var_int = 40;
        printf ("Address of variable \"var_int\": %p\n", &var_int);
}
```

Output:

```
Address of variable "var_int": 00394768
```

In the example above, we used the & operator to get the address of the variable.

If we extend the concept of address to a structure variable, where the structure variable itself contains many other variables, we can retrieve their addresses with the help of the "address of" operator.

Source code Ptr3.c

```
struct node{
int a;
int b;
};

int  main()
{
        struct node p;
        printf("Address of node = %p\n",&p);
        printf("Address of member variable a = %p\n", &(p.a));
        printf("Address of member variable b = %p\n", &(p.b));
        return 0;
}
```

```
Address of node = 003AFB00
Address of member variable a = 003AFB00
Address of member variable b = 003AFB04
```

Notice in the output above that the address of the first member and the second member in the data structures are very nearby. This means that for any number of member fields inside a structure, the addresses are allocated sequentially or nearby as per their sizes.

Pointer Declaration

Now you know how an address can be retrieved via the "address of" operator. Next, let's get a variable to store this address. This particular variable, which is capable of storing and operating on addresses of variables, is called a pointer variable. We will start with the declaration of the pointer variables. Below is the generic form through which we declare the pointer variables:

```
Datatype* variable_name;
```

Example 1: A pointer variable capable of pointing and storing addresses of primitive data types.

```
 int* intptr, char* charptr
```

The declaration of pointer variables involves a special operator called a dereference operator (*) which helps the compiler identify that it is a pointer variable. An associated data type informs the compiler about the kind of variable's data type address it holds. Both dereference and "address of" operators are unary in nature.

Example 2: Declaring pointers to aggregate data types (structures)

```
struct inner_node {
        int in_a;
        int in_b;
};

struct node{
        int *a;
        int *b;
        struct inner_node* in_node;
};
```

In the example above, `struct inner_node* in_node` is a pointer variable, where `struct inner_node` is a data type and the pointer variable's name is in_node. As seen above, we can have pointer variables as data members of structures.

Pointer Assignment

Like any other variable, pointer variables point to nothing when they are declared. It is the responsibility of the programmer to make it point to a valid memory address before dereferencing it. We will look into the meaning of dereferencing shortly.

Making a pointer variable point to a particular memory address can be done in two ways.

1. By assigning the variable's address with the help of an address of pointers (&).

```
int x = 40;
int *ptr;
ptr = &x;  // address of operator used to collect the address of variable x
```

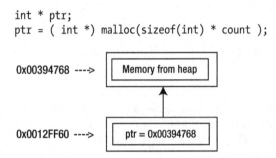

2. By making the pointer variable point to a dynamically allocated memory from the heap.

```
int * ptr;
ptr = ( int *) malloc(sizeof(int) * count );
```

In Case 1, the memory to store a value of 40 in variable *x* will be allocated during runtime, depending on the scope of the variable. Recall the memory layout sections in Chapter 1.

In Case 2, the memory to store a value is created explicitly using the malloc call, which returns memory from the heap area.

The programmer should keep in mind that any operation on a pointer variable should be done only if it is pointing to a valid memory address; otherwise this will result in a segmentation fault. If the segmentation fault occurs, it will lead the program to crash and eventually it will be stopped.

Size of Pointer Variables

The size of a variable is another important and critical aspect for a programmer. He should know how much a variable consumes when it is used. The size of any pointer variable can be 32-bit or 64-bit, depending on the platform. If a platform is 32-bit, the size of pointer variables (int *, char *, float *, and void *) will be 4 bytes. In fact, pointer variables that store the "address of" aggregate data types, such as arrays and structures, are also of size 4 bytes. Clearly, the memory address size of a pointer variable is 32 bits long.

The source code listed below shows the memory size occupied by pointer variables of different kinds (char *, int *, etc.).

Source code. Ptr4.c

```c
#include <stdio.h>
#include <conio.h>
int main()
{
        char c_var;
        int i_var;
        double d_var;
        char *char_ptr;
        int *int_ptr;
        double *double_ptr;
        char_ptr = &c_var;
        int_ptr = &i_var;
        double_ptr = &d_var;
        printf("Size of char pointer = %d value = %u\n", sizeof(char_ptr), char_ptr);
        printf("Size of integer pointer = %d value = %u\n", sizeof(int_ptr), int_ptr);
        printf("Size of double pointer = %d value = %u\n", sizeof(double_ptr),double_ptr);
        getch();
}
```

Output:

```
Size of char pointer = 4 value = 4061659
Size of integer pointer = 4 value = 4061644
Size of double pointer = 4 value = 4061628
```

It is interesting to verify the size consumed by a pointer variable that is pointing to structure variables. The following code illustrates this.

Source code. Ptr5.c

```c
#include <stdio.h>
#include <conio.h>
struct inner_node
{
        int in_a;
        int in_b;
};

struct node{
        int *a;
        int *b;
        struct inner_node* in_node;
};

int main()
{
        struct node *p;
        int *arrptr;
        int arr[10];
        arrptr = arr;
```

```
        printf("Size of pointer variable (struct node*) = %d\n",sizeof(struct node*));
        printf("Size of pointer variable pointing to int array = %d\n", sizeof(arrptr));
        return 0;
}
```

Output:

```
Size of pointer variable (struct node*) = 4
Size of pointer variable pointing to int array = 4
```

In the example above, the size of the data type struct node* is 4 bytes and conforms to the fact that the size of a memory address is always 4 bytes.

Pointer Dereferencing

Now that you can store and retrieve the address of a variable and store it to a pointer variable successfully, let's think about what you can do with this achievement. The pointer variable stores the address; to access the value stored at that address you use the "value at" operator (* to be precise). This particular technique is called pointer dereferencing. This is also called indirection in some texts. You will see the advantages of using pointer variables in the coming sections.

Every variable is used to store a value, and this rule is also applicable for pointer variables. The value of a pointer variable is the address of some memory location. Once we store a memory address in a pointer variable, we should be able to find the value stored at this location. Let's see how this is done with pointer dereferencing.

We need to use the dereferencing operator (*) to get the value stored at some memory location. This operator is also called "value at" operator. Consider the following code:

```
int x = 10; /* value 10 stored at some memory location */
int *ptr = &x; /* now pointer variable "ptr" is pointing to the memory location x = 10 */
printf("Address of variable \"x\" = %p\n", &x); /* prints the address of memory location x */
printf("Address of variable \"x\" = %p\n", ptr); /*prints the address of memory location x with the
help of "ptr" variable, whose value is memory location "x" */
printf("Value of variable \"x\" = %d\n", x); /* prints the value of variable x */
printf("Value stored at address ptr = %p is %d\n", ptr, *ptr); /* prints the value at memory
location of x with the help of value at operator (*ptr)      */
```

Essentially the value of variable ptr and the value of the expression (&x) evaluates to one thing: a memory location of variable x, since ptr is pointing to x right now.

To get the value stored at some memory location, we use the dereferencing operator (*). Therefore, the expressions *ptr, *(&x), and x will evaluate to one and the same thing: 10.

■ **Tip** Before dereferencing any pointer variable make sure that it points to a valid memory address, as in Example A in Figure 2-1; otherwise segmentation fault will occur. The cause of this error is due to an invalid memory access, as in Example B of Figure 2-1.

Example A

int x = 10;

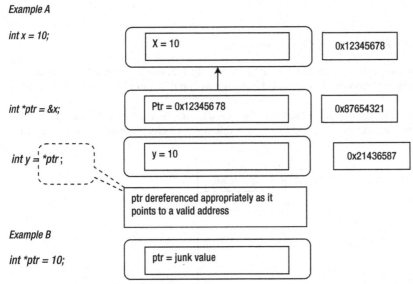

int *ptr = &x;

int y = *ptr ;

ptr dereferenced appropriately as it
points to a valid address

Example B

int *ptr = 10;

ptr = junk value

int y = *ptr; // At this point the program will crash, as we are trying to access a memory location which is not valid

Figure 2-1. *Pointer variables pointing to a valid memory address and an invalid one*

In the first line of Example B, we are trying to keep the value 10 at a location that is not valid since the variable ptr is not pointing to a valid memory location.

To make this program work correctly we need to make the ptr variable point to a valid memory location. The following code illustrates the appropriate method to do this:

```
int count = 1; //"count" variable will be used to allocate one memory location of size integer type
int *ptr = (int *) malloc ( sizeof(int) * count );
```

Now the ptr variable points to a valid memory location.

```
*ptr = 10; //At this point we are assigning a value to the memory location where "ptr" is pointing to
free(ptr) ; // At this point we freed the memory pointed to by the variable "ptr"
*ptr = 20; // Again at this point the program will throw a segmentation error, because we are trying
to access a memory which has already been freed.
```

Basic Usage of Pointer

You have seen how pointers are declared and initialized. We will now look into the most basic usage of pointers, or rather the advantage of using pointers. Functions and parameters go hand in hand. With pointer variables we have a lot of luxury to manipulate any memory value with the help of indirection. To understand this section, it would be a good idea to refresh the lifecycle, scope of the variable, and stack segment from Chapter 1.

Pass by Value

Functions are capable of receiving information from the caller and returning results back to the caller. This technique is the most basic form of information passing among functions.

Function Signature

```
int function_name( int param1, int param2, int param3 .....);
```

In the declaration of the function above, the parameters int param1, int param2, and int param3 are called input parameters. The return type of this function declaration is int, which tells that this function will return a value of type integer to the caller function.

In this particular technique, only the values are being passed to the called function. After the values are passed, these values are copied onto the respective stack of the called function. Similarly, the exact process is repeated for the returned value of the called function.

```
void calling_function(void)
{
int t1, t2, t3;
t1 = 10;
t2 = 20;
t3 = called_function(t1, t2);
}
```

Local copy of the calling_function
t1 = 10
t2 = 20
t3 = 30

```
int called_function(int x, int y)
{
int t1, t2, t3;
t1 = x;
t2 = y;
t3 = t1 + t2;
return t3;
}
```

Local copy of the called_function
t1 = 10
t2 = 20
t3 = 30

Pass by Reference

This is another technique of passing information among functions. Pass by reference is used to pass the memory address of variables rather than the value itself.

Function Signature

```
int* function_name( int* param);
```

In the function declaration above, the input parameter param is of int*, which is expecting to receive the address of an integer variable from the calling function. And this function will also be returning the address of an integer variable to the calling function.

```
void calling_function(void)
{
int t1;
int *t2;
t1 = 10;
t2 = called_function(&t1);
}


int* called_function(int* x)
{
int t2;
int *t1;
int *t3;
t1 = x;
t2 = 10;
t3 = (int*)malloc(sizeof(int));
t3 = *t1 + t2;
return &t3;
}
```

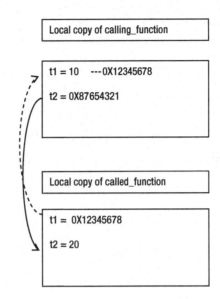

In the case above, only the address of a variable is passed to the called function, which then is copied to the stack. This technique has two advantages as compared to the former technique.

1. **Amount of data being copied:** Although the copying of the parameter is carried out in this case as well (i.e., the copying of the memory address), the amount of information that is copied will always be 4 bytes. In the example above, the amount (size) of information that is passed is the same.

Case 1: Pass by value

```
struct data
{
int x;
int y;
};
void func(struct data v1)
{
struct data v2 = v1;
}
int main()
{
struct data var;
var.x = 10;
var.y = 20;
func( var );
return 0;
}
```

In the example above, the size of the variable struct data is 8 bytes. Since pass by value is used, 8 bytes are copied onto the stack of the called function func.

Case 2: Pass by reference

```
struct data
{
int x;
int y;
};
void func(struct data* v1)
{
struct data *v2 = v1;
}
int main()
{
struct data var;
var->x = 10;
var->y = 20;
func(& var );
return 0;
}
```

In the example above, the size of the parameter is 4 bytes since we passed the pointer to the structure variable.

2. **Accessibility of variables:** The pass by reference technique makes it possible to manipulate the local variables of a function from a different function.

Pointers and Constants

You may have heard of the keyword const and used it in programming. A normal variable use of const has one meaning. The value assigned during initialization will never change throughout the lifetime of the variable in its scope. However, the use of the pointers and constants together can have a varied affect.

Constant Pointer Variable

A constant pointer is a pointer variable that is meant to point to only one memory address. Therefore, the value of the pointer variable cannot be changed.

Declaration of constant pointer: `<pointer type*> const <variable name>`
Example: `int* const ptr1, char* const ptr2;`
Here are the rules for using constant pointers.

1. Constant pointer variables must be initialized during declaration.

Source code. Ptr6.c

```
int main()
{
int num = 10;
int* const ptr1 = &num;   //Initialization of const ptr
printf("Value stored at pointer = %d\n",*ptr1);
}
```

2. Once initialized, the const pointer should not point to any other memory address.

Source code. Ptr7.c

```
#1. int main()
#2. {
#3. int num1 = 10;
#4. int num2 = 20;
#5. int* const ptr1 = &num1;  //Initialization of const ptr

#6. ptr1 = &num2; // can't do this
#7. printf("Value stored at pointer = %d\n",*ptr1);
#8. }
```

Mem addr	values
0x123456	num1 = 10
0x654321	num2 = 20
0x111122	Const Ptr1 = 0x123456

Mem addr	values
0x123456	num1 = 10
0x654321	num2 = 20
0x111122	Const Ptr1 = 0x654321

In the program above, the constant pointer variable ptr1 is initialized at line #5 and is pointing to the memory address of the variable int num1. At line #6, the program is trying to make the constant pointer variable ptr1 point to the memory address of the variable int num2. When this particular piece of code is compiled, the compiler will throw a compilation error.

Pointer to Constant Variable

A pointer to a constant variable is a concept where the value of a pointer variable (i.e., a memory address of a non-constant variable) should not modify the value at that particular memory address. Different pointers could point to that specific variable.

Declaration of constant pointer: const<pointer type*> <variable name>
Example: *const int* ptr1, const char* ptr2;*

Source code. Ptr8.c

```
#1. int main()
#2. {
#3. int num1 = 10;
#4. const int* ptr1;

#5. int* ptr2;
#6. ptr1 = &num1;


#7. *ptr1 = 20; //can't do this
#8. num1 = 20; //can be done
#9. printf("Value stored at pointer = %d\n",*ptr1);
#10. }
```

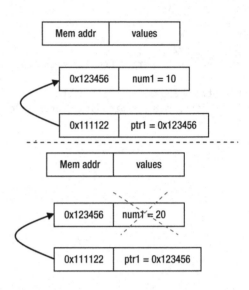

When we try to compile the code above, the compiler will throw a compilation error because of line #7.

Constant Pointer to a Constant Variable

A constant pointer to a constant variable is a concept where a pointer variable is constant; in other words, the pointer variable will only point to a memory address where it is initialized, and later the pointer should not point to any other memory location. Additionally, the value stored at that particular address should not be modified by that particular pointer. In summary, we cannot change the value of a pointer variable and we cannot modify the value stored at that address.

Declaration of constant pointer: const<pointer type*> const <variable name>
Example: const int*const ptr1, const char* const ptr2;

Source code. Ptr9.c

```
#1. int main()
#2. {
#3. int num1 = 10;
#4. int num2 = 20;
#5. const int* ptr1 = &num1;
#6. int* ptr2;
#7. *ptr1 = 20; //cannot change the value that the  const pointer is pointing to
#8. num1 = 20; //can be done
#9. ptr1 = &num2; //cannot change the constant pointer's value (i.e. - constant pointer should //not
point to any other memory address once initialized
#10.printf("Value stored at pointer = %d\n",*ptr1);
#11. }
```

When we try to compile the code above, the compiler will throw a compilation error because of line #7 and line #9.

Multilevel Pointers

Until now, you have seen and worked with one level of indirection. You may have thought about the possibility of multilevel indirection. As you saw earlier, pointer variables are able to store the memory address of other variables, and it is possible to extend this notion further. The address of a pointer variable itself can be stored in any other pointer variable.

The variable used for storing an address of a pointer variable is called a pointer to pointer variable. We can extend this more, such as pointer to pointer to pointer variable and so forth.

Pointer to a Pointer Variable

We will now discuss the second level of pointer indirection. Consider the following piece of code:

```
int a = 10;
int *ptr = &a;
```

In this code, we have declared an integer variable *a* and an integer pointer variable ptr, which is pointing to that integer variable. Now we will see how to store the address of this integer pointer variable into another pointer variable. To be able to store the address of a pointer variable into another variable, we need a different kind of variable.

Declaration: <data type >** <variable_name>

The number of asterisks depends on the level of indirection. We keep on increasing the number of asterisks as the level of indirection increases.

```
int a = 10;
int *ptr = &a;
int **ptr1 = &ptr;
```

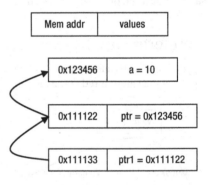

Source code. Ptr10.c

```
int main()
{
        int num = 10;
        int *ptr = &num;
        int **mptr = &ptr;
        printf("Value of var num = %d\n", num);
        printf("Value of var num = %d\n", *ptr);
        printf("Value of var num = %d\n", **mptr);

        printf("Address of var num = %p\n", &num);
        printf("Address of var num = %p\n", ptr);
        printf("Address of var num = %p\n", *mptr);

        printf("Address of pointer var ptr = %p\n",&ptr);
        printf("Address of pointer var ptr = %p\n",mptr);
        printf("Address of pointer var mptr = %p\n",&mptr);

        return 0;
}
```

Understanding a Cryptic Pointer Expression

Understanding pointer expressions becomes cryptic due to the many ways a pointer address can be dereferenced. In this section, we will focus on segregating the equivalent expressions and thus understanding these expressions more easily. You may find this section iterative, but it is a good idea to collate all of the information together.

We will begin by considering the case of one level of indirection. In all further discussions, we will consider an integer variable with its value initialized to 10 and its storage at memory location 0x0001. We will see equivalence of these expressions with two scenarios (referencing and dereferencing).

Referencing

```
int val = 10;
```

Varname/Addr	Value
val/0x0001	10

```
int *ptrvar = &val;
```

Varname/Addr	Value	Varname/Addr	Value
		val/0x0001	10
ptrvar/0x0005	0x0001		

Since the pointer variable ptrvar is storing the address of the variable val, and the expression &val yields the same value, both of these expressions are equivalent. Therefore, we can say ptrvar == &val.

Dereferencing

As you know, to dereference we use the "value at" (*) operator. If we try to use this operator on a pointer variable, it will yield the value stored at the memory address that is stored in that location.

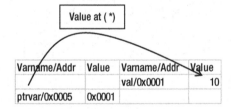

Varname/Addr	Value	Varname/Addr	Value
		val/0x0001	10
ptrvar/0x0005	0x0001		

```
*ptrvar == 10
```

Also, in the section referenced above, we saw that ptrvar == &val. We can use the "address of" operator expression to yield the same value.

```
*(&val) == 10
```

Therefore, the following expressions are equivalent: *ptrvar == *(&val) == 10.

Now, let's do the same exercise with two levels of indirection. We will use the same two variables that we used above, and a new variable to store the address of an integer pointer variable.

a.   `int val = 10;`

b.   `int *ptrvar = &val;`

c.   `int **ptrptrvar = &ptrvar;`

Let's start with referencing.

Referencing

For the first two variables, the schematic memory diagram will be the same as what we drew earlier in the one level indirection case. For the third variable that is a pointer to a pointer variable of type integer, refer to the following schematic diagram.

`int **ptrptrvar = &ptrvar;`

Varname/Addr	Value	Varname/Addr	Value	Varname/Addr	Value
				val/0x0001	10
		ptrvar/0x0005	0x0001		
ptrptrvar/0x0009	0x0005				

The variable `ptrptrvar` is a pointer to pointer variable that is storing the address of a pointer variable. Therefore, we verify the expression `ptrptrvar == &ptrvar`.

Dereferencing

In this section, we will apply the value at operator to the top most level and then we will see how the meanings of the expressions change.

`*ptrptrvar == ptrvar == 0x0001`

Since `ptrptrvar == &ptrvar`, we can obtain the same value by another equivalent expression.

`*(&ptrvar) == 0x0001`

Therefore, `*ptrptrvar == ptrvar == *(&ptrvar) == 0x0001`.

Now, we will apply the second level of indirection: **ptrptrvar*, this expression will yield the value 10. We can write `**ptrptrvar == 10`.

In the expression above, if we try to replace the `*ptrptrvar` part, we can substitute its equivalent expression mentioned above to get the same result. Therefore, `**ptrptrvar == *(ptrvar) == *(*(&ptrvar) ) == 10`.

The same concept that we discussed above is explained with the help of Figure 2-1.

Figure 2-2 gives a visual representation (with reference to the example above) of how a pointer to a variable and pointers to pointer variables are used. To gain the indirect access to an actual variable, we can use multiples of a "value at" operator (&) or combination of a "value at" operator (&) and the "address of" operator (*).

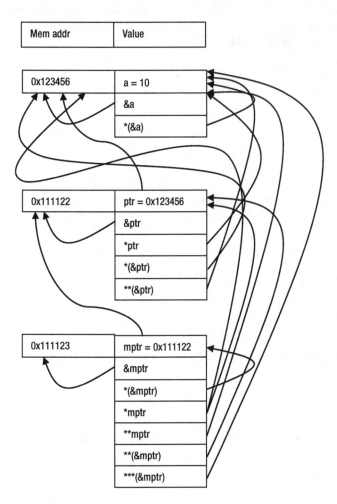

Mem addr	Value
0x123456	a = 10
	&a
	*(&a)
0x111122	ptr = 0x123456
	&ptr
	*ptr
	*(&ptr)
	**(&ptr)
0x111123	mptr = 0x111122
	&mptr
	*(&mptr)
	*mptr
	**mptr
	**(&mptr)
	***(&mptr)

Figure 2-2. *Pointer expressions*

Summary

In this chapter we covered the basics of pointers and their usage. The goal of this chapter is that you understand the concept of referencing and dereferencing. You should concentrate more on this concept with multilevel indirections. Pointers with structure variables are covered in very minimalist form in this chapter; an upcoming chapter is dedicated solely to understanding pointers when they are used for structure type variables.

In the next chapter, we will look into more advanced concepts of pointer arithmetic. We will also cover the use of pointers with arrays.

■ ■ ■

CHAPTER 3

Pointer Arithmetic and Single Dimension Arrays

Arithmetic operations can be performed on most, but not all variables. Fortunately, these operations can also be performed on pointer variables. This is one of the most important uses of pointers, in addition to referencing and dereferencing the memory addresses.

This navigation is achieved with the help of some limited arithmetic operations provided by C language.

When visualizing memory as laid out in consecutive blocks, the natural thought process points us to the array data type because an array's indices are laid out consecutively, too. The usage of pointer arithmetic comes along with the arrays of different data types. In this chapter, you will learn the details of pointer arithmetic and its usage with arrays.

Array Memory Layout

The array is one of most basic programming constructs. I am sure that many readers have used it in their programs already. An array by definition is a collection of similar data types, and when it is laid out in memory, they take consecutive memory locations that can be accessed with the help of their indices.

Below is the memory dump of an integer type array, which specifies the array name a along with an index, its memory location, and the value at that location.

Array Name – Memory Address – Value:

```
a[0] 4455240 0 a[1] 4455244 1 a[2] 4455248 2 a[3] 4455252 3 a[4] 4455256 4
a[5] 4455260 5 a[6] 4455264 6 a[7] 4455268 7 a[8] 4455272 8
a[9] 4455276 9 a[10] 4455280 10 a[11] 4455284 11 a[12] 4455288 12
a[13] 4455292 13 a[14] 4455296 14 a[15] 4455300 15 a[16] 4455304 16
a[17] 4455308 17 a[18] 4455312 18 a[19] 4455316 19 a[20] 4455320 20
a[21] 4455324 21 a[22] 4455328 22 a[23] 4455332 23 a[24] 4455336 24
a[25] 4455340 25 a[26] 4455344 26 a[27] 4455348 27 a[28] 4455352 28
a[29] 4455356 29 a[30] 4455360 30 a[31] 4455364 31
```

The code below represents the memory dump shown above.

Source code Ptr1.c

```c
#include <stdio.h>
int main()
{
        int iArray[32];
        int i;
        for(i = 0; i<32; i++)
        {
                iArray[i] = i;
        }
        for(i = 0; i<32; i++)
        {
                printf("a[%d] %u %d ",i, &iArray[i], iArray[i]);
                if((i%4 == 0) && (i != 0))
                        printf("\n");
        }
        getch();
}
```

If the memory dump shown above is analyzed closely, you can see that each neighboring array index shares consecutive memory locations. For example, the 0th array index, a[0], has memory location of 4455240, and the first array index, a[1], shares the next neighboring memory location of 4455244, and so on.

If we subtract a previous consecutive memory location from the latter (&a[1] - &a[0] = 4), we get 4 as a result. We get the value of 4 because an integer takes the size of 1 word (32 bits/4 bytes) in the memory. Therefore, the variable a[0] is placed in the memory from the address 4455240 to 4455243.

Similarly, the next index, a[1], is laid out from next available memory location of 4455244 to 4455247.

The equivalent memory dump with hexadecimal representations is shown below:

0x0043FB48 00 00 00 00 01 00 00 00 02 00 00 00 03 00 00 00 04 00 00 00 05 00 00 00 06 00 00

00 07 00 00 00 08 00 00 00 09 00 00 00 0a 00 00 00 ....

0x0043FB74 0b 00 00 00 0c 00 00 00 0d 00 00 00 0e 00 00 00 0f 00 00 00 10 00 00 00 11 00 00

00 12 00 00 00 13 00 00 00 14 00 00 00 15 00 00 00 ....

0x0043FBA0 16 00 00 00 17 00 00 00 18 00 00 00 19 00 00 00 1a 00 00 00 1b 00 00 00 1c 00 00

00 1d 00 00 00 1e 00 00 00 1f 00 00 00

The highlighted circle above points to the $a[1]^{th}$ index of the array at location 0x0043FB4C, which starts after the fourth byte from the start of array index and the value at that address is 1. If you examine it carefully, you can find how the value of 1 (0x0001) is stored at that location. The format used here is called little endian.

Endianness

Endianness describes the format/layout in which data will be stored in memory. Load/Store instructions read data from memory and write data back into memory from registers after some instructions are executed on the data.

While storing and loading, the CPU must take care of the endianness of the underlying format that the hardware follows.

Endianness is of two kinds: big and little. The size of a word is 4 bytes/32 bits. Let's assume that we intend to store a value of 0x1234 into a variable. You will see below how this particular value gets stored in either of the situations.

As shown below, we have 4 bytes in place (1, 2, 3, 4) for 0x1234. In case of the big endian, the most significant byte gets stored in the first available location, and then the next most significant byte gets stored in next available location, and so on.

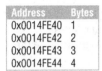

Address	Bytes
0x0014FE40	1
0x0014FE42	2
0x0014FE43	3
0x0014FE44	4

Big endian

In the case of little endian, the least significant byte gets stored in the first available location, and then the next least significant byte gets stored in the next available location, and so on.

Address	Bytes
0x0014FE40	4
0x0014FE42	3
0x0014FE43	2
0x0014FE44	1

Little endian

Analyze the output of the following program to get a better understanding of the concept of endianness.

Source code Ptr2.c

```c
#include <stdio.h>
#define BIG_ENDIAN 0
#define LITTLE_ENDIAN 1
int endian()
{
        short int word = 0x0001;
        char *byte = (char *) &word;
        return (byte[0] ? LITTLE_ENDIAN : BIG_ENDIAN);
}
int main(int argc, char* argv[])
{
        int value;
        value = endian();
        if (value == 1)
                printf("The machine is Little Endian\n");
        else
                printf("The machine is Big Endian\n");
        return 0;
}
```

Pointer Arithmetic

This section introduces the concept of pointer arithmetic, and this will form one of the very important building blocks in understanding the functionality of pointers.

The operators that can be used to perform pointer arithmetic are as follows:

+ +

- -

-

+

Note that the division (/) and multiplication (*) operators are not allowed here.

As explained in the first section, arrays are laid out consecutively in memory. Each array element resides consecutively in memory blocks that can be accessed with an array index. Consider the picture below to visualize the notion of pointer arithmetic.

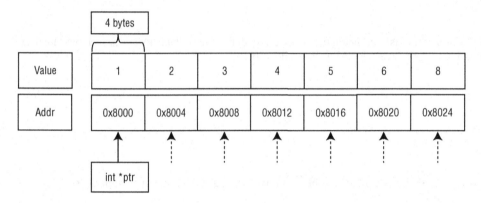

Since every index location is a memory address that holds the value of some data type, we can make a pointer variable of similar data type to point to a particular index.

For example, int arr[10]; // array of type integer which can hold 10 integers.

```
int* ptr; //  an integer to pointer
ptr = arr; // This will point to first index of the array element.
```

Pointer Addition

The + operator is used to perform addition. Consider the figure above where the pointer variable ptr is pointing to the 0th index of the array at location 0x8000. We can perform pointer addition in the following way:

ptr = ptr + 1;

This line makes the variable ptr point to the next integer location of 0x8004. This arithmetic operation on pointers is of a special kind. Generally, one would expect that the value of ptr variable after the addition would be 0x8001 as per the normal additive rule. But, in the case of pointer arithmetic, any addition to a pointer variable makes the pointer variable point to the address of the numeric value in the expression which is evaluated by multiplying the numeric value and the size of data type. In the example above, we are dealing with arrays and an integer pointer. Each integer variable takes four bytes in memory.

0th Index				1st Index			
Byte 1	Byte 2	Byte 3	Byte 4	Byte 1	Byte 2	Byte 3	Byte 4
0x8000	0x8001	0x8002	0x8003	0x8004	0x8005	0x8006	0x8007

ptr

Whenever pointer variable points to a data type, it will always point to the location of first byte of the data type's address in the memory location.

And whenever a pointer variable is incremented by one, it will point to the next integer's location (i.e., it will jump to the start of the next integer's location, four bytes ahead in this case, and not to the next byte's location).

Source code Ptr3.c

```
#include <stdio.h>
int main(int argc, char* argv[])
{
        int i = 0;
        int data = 9;
        int *iptr;
        char *cptr;
        iptr = &data;
        cptr = (char*)&data;
        printf("value of data = %d hex value = %x\n", data, data);
        printf("Address of data = %p\n", &data);
        printf("Integer pointer pointing at %p\n", iptr);
        printf("Character pointer pointing at %p\n", cptr);
        printf("Printing address of all the four bytes of variable int data\n");
        for(i = 0;i<4;i++)
        {
        printf("address = %p value = %x\n",cptr, *cptr);
        cptr++;
        }
        return 0;
        }
```

Output:

```
value of data = 9 hex value = 9
Address of data = 0039FAD8
Integer pointer pointing at 0039FAD8
Character pointer pointing at 0039FAD8
Printing address of all the four bytes of variable int data
address = 0039FAD8 value = 9
address = 0039FAD9 value = 0
address = 0039FADA value = 0
address = 0039FADB
value = 0
```

From the output above, you can easily see that int variable data with value 9 is spanning through four bytes, starting from address 0x0039FAD8 to 0X0039FADB. The char pointer is used here to illustrate this fact.

So, what makes pointer variable to jump to next fourth byte from its current location, rather than jumping to next immediate byte's location?

Let's examine the assembler's output from following statements:

a) Ptr = Ptr + 1;

Assembler output:

```
mov     eax, DWORD PTR _Ptr$[ebp]
add     eax, 4
mov     DWORD PTR _Ptr$[ebp], eax
```

Since the statement is trying to increment the pointer variable's value and point it only to the adjacent integer variable, the second line in the assembler's output add   eax, 4 reveals that pointer is added a value of 4 and that's why it points to the next fourth byte.

b) Ptr = Ptr + 2;

Assembler output:

```
mov     eax, DWORD PTR _Ptr$[ebp]
add     eax, 8
mov     DWORD PTR _Ptr$[ebp], eax
```

Again, add eax, 8 reveals that the pointer is being added a value of 8 and not 2. The compiler performs the following conversion during the pointer arithmetic:

```
<Pointer-variable> = <Pointer-variable> + <increment value >
```

TO

```
<Pointer-variable> = <Pointer-variable> + <size of data type of Pointer variable > * <increment
value>
```

■ **Note**   Adding an offset to pointer variable is very much legal operation, but adding a pointer variable to another pointer variable is not allowed.

```
Ptr1 = Ptr1 + Ptr2; // illegal
```

Pointer Subtraction

The - operator is used to perform subtraction. Consider figure below, where pointer variable ptr is pointing to the first index of the array at location 0x8004; we can perform pointer subtraction as shown.

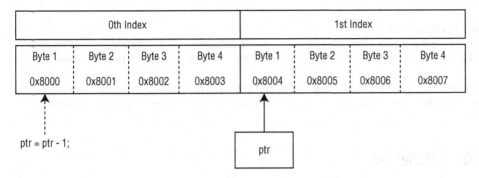

The line ptr = ptr -1 makes the variable ptr point to the previous integer location, 0x8000.
<u>Assembler output:</u>

```
mov     eax, DWORD PTR _iptr$[ebp]
sub     eax, 4
mov     DWORD PTR _iptr$[ebp], eax
```

Since the statement is trying to decrement it only to adjacent integer variable, the second line in assembler's output of sub eax, 4 reveals that the pointer is subtracted by the value of 4 and that is why it points to the previous 4th byte, 0x8000.

The compiler performs the following conversion during the pointer arithmetic.

```
<Pointer-variable> = <Pointer-variable> - <decrement value >
```

TO

```
<Pointer-variable> = <Pointer-variable> - <size of data type of Pointer variable > * <decrement value>
```

Subtracting Two Pointer Variables

Consider the following code snippet:

Source code Ptr4.c

```
int main(int argc, char* argv[])
{
        int data[4] = {1,2,3,4};
        int *iptr1;
        int *iptr2;
        int val;
        iptr1 = &data[0];
        iptr2 = &data[1];
        val = iptr2 - iptr1;
        printf("Distance between the two addresses = %d\n", val);
        return 0;
}
```

Output:

Distance between the two addresses = 1

When two pointer variables are pointing to separate locations within consecutive memory addresses of an array and then they are subtracted from each other, the difference represents the number of elements present between the two pointer variables.

In code snippet above , `int* ptr1` is pointing to the 0th index and `int*ptr2` is pointing to the first index. When both the variables are subtracted from each other, it evaluates to 1 because only one element is present between these two consecutive locations.

Comparing Two Pointer Variables

Consider the following code snippet:

Source code Ptr5.c

```
#include <stdio.h>
int main(int argc, char* argv[])
{
        int data[4] = {1,2,3,4};
        int *iptr1;
        int *iptr2;
        iptr1 = &data[0];
        iptr2 = &data[1];
        if(iptr1 == iptr2)
                printf("Address of iptr1 is equal to address of iptr2\n);
        if(iptr1 > iptr2)
                printf("Address of iptr1 is greater than address of iptr2\n");
        else
                printf("Address of iptr1 is smaller than address of iptr2\n");
        return 0;
}
```

The pointer variables can be tested for equality and inequality, as shown above.

Arrays Explored

To understand the usage and correlation between pointers and arrays, we need to explore the meaning of some typical syntaxes that go along with array variables.

To reiterate, an array is a set of consecutive memory locations that stores the values of the data type that is augmented in its definition.

```
int arr_var[100];
```

To access the individual data elements within the array, we use subscripts notation, as follows:

```
Array name [subscript] / arr_var [ i ].
```

The variable name of an array is equivalent to the address of the 0th location of that particular array. So we may say that the expression below is equivalent and yields the same result: the address of the 0th index of the array.

arr_var ≈ &arr_var [0]

If we increment it with an offset, we can iterate through the consecutive addresses of data elements within that array, as follows:

```
arr_var + 1 // address of 1st index
arr_var + 2 //address of 2nd index location.
```

To generalize this, we could say

arr_var + offset ≈ &arr_var [offset] ➤ expression refers to address

   AND

*(arr_var + offset) ≈ arr_var[offset] ➤ expression refers to value

Source code Ptr6.c

```c
#include <stdio.h>
int main(int argc, char* argv[])
{
        int arr[4] = {1,2,3,4};
        printf("Address of 0th index = %p\n", arr);
        printf("Address of 0th index = %p\n", &arr[0]);
        return 0;
}
```

   Output:

```
Address of 0th index = 003AFAAC
Address of 0th index = 003AFAAC
```

As you can see, the name of an array variable acts like a pointer to the 0th index of the array. If we add offset, then it behaves like a pointer variable.

Source code Ptr7.c

```c
#include <stdio.h>
int main(int argc, char* argv[])
{
        int arr[4] = {1,2,3,4};
        int *iptr;
        iptr = &arr[0] + 2; //pointing to the 2nd element
        printf("Address of 2nd index = %p\n", iptr);
        iptr = &arr[2]; //pointing to the 2nd element
        printf("Address of 2nd index = %p\n", iptr);
        return 0;
}
```

Output:

```
Address of second index = 003CF83C
Address of second index = 003CF83C
```

Note that arr_var[i] is an element at the ith location of the array variable. Therefore *(arr_var + i) will yield us the same element as the previous expression, an element at i^th index.

Source code Ptr8.c

```c
#include <stdio.h>
int main(int argc, char* argv[])
{
        int arr[4] = {1,2,3,4};
        printf("Address of 0th index = %p\n", arr);
        printf("Address of 0th index = %p\n", &arr[0]);
        return 0;
}
```

Output:
```
Address of 0th index = 003AFAAC
Address of 0th index = 003AFAAC
Value at 0th index = 1
Value at 0th index = 1
```

■ **Note** Although the name of an array variable represents the address of 0th index for that array, it is forbidden to change its value (in other words, make it point it to some other location).

```c
int arr_var[ 5];
arr_var = arr_var + 1; // this is not allowed since this expression is trying to shift the pointer
location via array name to the next integer variable's address.
arr_var ++; //illegal statement, as it is trying to change the starting address of an array variable
```

Dynamic Array

There are situations in which we don't know the number of elements that needs to be stored in an array at the time of definition. During runtime, these elements can increase or decrease in number. So, if a programmer intends to store these elements in an array, the array needs to be dynamic so its size can be changed during runtime.

You have learned how an array is declared:

```c
int arr_stat[10];
```

This declaration makes sure that the size of array is known at the compile time, which eventually can be called static in nature. The size of this kind of array cannot be changed during runtime.

Pointers can help us manipulate memory regions and achieve the intended behavior such that memory could be increased or decreased as needed. To achieve this, we use pointers and heap. The malloc() function call helps us allocate memory in heap. Let's take a small code snippet to visualize the scenario of an on-demand memory requirement.

Requirement: When a user inserts data, the memory gets adjusted in size and the data element should get stored appropriately. When user deletes data, the memory should get freed.

Initial assumptions: There is no data to store.

Source code Ptr9.c

```
#include <stdio.h>
#include <malloc.h>
int *ptr = NULL;
static int count = 0;
void insert(int data)
{
#1      if(ptr == NULL)
#2      {
#3              ptr = (int*)malloc(sizeof(int)); //allocating space from heap for 1st data
#4              ptr[0] = data; //accessing memory address with array notation to store data
#5      }
#6      else
#7      {
#8              ptr = (int*)realloc(ptr, sizeof(int)*(count+1)); //Increasing the size of memory to
#9              //accomodate new integer
#10             ptr[count] = data; //accessing memory address with array notation to store data
#11     }
#12     count++;
}
void show()
{
        int i = 0;
        for(i = 0; i< count; i++)
        {
                printf("%d\n", ptr[i]);
        }
}
int main(int argc, char* argv[])
{
        int c = 0;
        int data;
        while( c != 3 )
        {
                printf("Insert choice\n");
                printf("1 to insert data\n");
                printf("2 to Show data\n");
                printf("3 to quit data\n");
                scanf("%d",&c);
                if( c == 3)
                        break;
                switch(c)
                {
                        case 1:
                                printf("Data = \n");
                                scanf("%d",&data);
                                insert(data);
                                break;
```

```
                        case 2:
                                printf("Data in array\n");
                                show();
                                        break;
        }
    }
        return 0;
}
```

In the code snippet above, the insert(int data) function (line #1 through #5) inserts the first element. The memory is allocated using malloc() function call and the pointer variable ptr is made to point to the memory location returned from the heap. In this code, only one data element is added at a time, so only one memory space is required for the specific data.

Line numbers #6 through #12 increases the space allocated to incorporate the new data element. At line #8, the realloc() function call is used that actually creates the new space for the data, which will be pointed by variable ptr. The realloc() function call has additional parameter, which it takes to increase the size.

Variable count is used to keep track of the number of elements currently inserted. Note that the size to be allocated should be one extra than the currently inserted element.

Array of Pointers

Array of pointers by definition is meant to store pointer variables in its consecutive location. Every location in this array will contain memory address of some data in memory.

Declaration of array of pointer -- **<data type*> <variable name> [no. of elements]**
Ex. int * arr_ptr[10] // pointer to 10 integer variable

Source code Ptr10.c

```c
#include <stdio.h>
int main(int argc, char* argv[])
{
        int arr[4] = {1,2,3,4};
        int* arr_ptr[4];
        int i;
        for(i = 0; i<4; i++)
        {
                arr_ptr[i] = arr + i;
        }
        printf("Address of (arr) array element\n");
        for(i = 0; i<4; i++)
        {
                printf("Address of %d index = %p\n",i, arr + i);
        }
        printf("Value of (arr_ptr) array of pointer element \n");
        for(i = 0; i<4; i++)
        {
                printf("Value of %d index = %p\n",i, arr_ptr[i]);
        }
        return 0;
}
```

Output:
```
Address of (arr) array element
Address of 0 index = 003CFD64
Address of 1 index = 003CFD68
Address of 2 index = 003CFD6C
Address of 3 index = 003CFD70
Value of (arr_ptr) array of pointer element
Value of 0 index = 003CFD64
Value of 1 index = 003CFD68
Value of 2 index = 003CFD6C
Value of 3 index = 003CFD70
```

If we analyze the output above, the array of pointers arr_ptr contains the address of each element of the array arr.

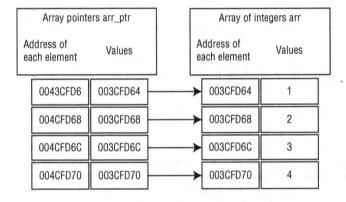

Pointer to Array

By definition, it is a pointer variable that points to an array.

Declaration of pointer to array -- **<data type> (* <variable name>) [no. of elements]**
int (* ptr2arr) [4]; // it is a pointer to an array of 4 integers
Like any other pointer variable, it can point to only one location at a time.

Source code Ptr11.c

```c
#include <stdio.h>
int main(int argc, char* argv[])
{
        int arr[4] = {1,2,3,4};
        int (* ptr2arr)[4];
        int i;
        int *ptr = arr;
        ptr2arr = &arr;
        for(i = 0; i<4; i++)
        {
        printf("address of array = %p\n", arr + i);
        }
```

```
        printf("Value at = %d\n",*(ptr2arr[0] + 1));
        for(i = 0; i<4; i++)
        {
        printf("Value at %p = %d\n",(ptr2arr[0] + i),*(ptr2arr[0] + i));
        }
        return 0;
}
```

Output:

```
address of array = 001BFB90
address of array = 001BFB94
address of array = 001BFB98
address of array = 001BFB9C
Value at 001BFB90 = 1
Value at 001BFB94 = 2
Value at 001BFB98 = 3
Value at 001BFB9C = 4
```

In the code snippet above, ptr2arr is a pointer to array, where the array that it is pointing to is capable of storing four data elements of integer type.

Summary

This chapter explored the details of pointer arithmetic. You learned how pointer arithmetic helps in iterating over the array index. Subsequent chapters show different kinds of iterations you can perform with the help of pointers, enabling you to iterate and traverse through dynamic data structures such as linked lists.

The next chapter covers the use of pointers on strings. You will see how the pointers can be used to manipulate the string values.

CHAPTER 4

■ ■ ■

Pointers and Strings

As software developers, we could be writing code for a user-application or complex device drivers, and we use strings very frequently. A string by definition is a sequence of characters. It is stored as an array of bytes. A special string terminating character is used to mark the end of a string. The terminating character is denoted by the escape sequence, '\0'.

This chapter explains how a character array or string is represented in memory and how memory is allocated to store character strings. This chapter focuses on the use of pointers as a tool to manipulate the strings. Later sections discuss the common operations performed on these strings in detail.

The following are the basic operations that can be performed on strings:

1. Comparing two strings.

2. String copying.

3. Finding lengths of strings.

4. Finding a substring within a string

Let's start the chapter by defining a string variable with an initializer in different ways. We will discuss the meaning of these definitions later.

```
char *strptr = "Hello";
char strarray1[] = "Hello";
char strarray2[6] = "Hello";
char strarray3[4] = { 'a', 'b', 'c', 'd' };
```

String Layout in Memory

Typically, a character array or string will be stored in contiguous memory locations, as depicted in Figure 4-1.

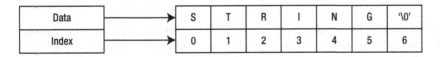

Figure 4-1. *String's memory layout*

Note that there are six data elements in the array, but it takes one extra space to store the terminating character.

```c
char arr1[7] = "STRING";
```

Data		S	T	R	I	N	G	'\0'
Index		0	1	2	3	4	5	6

In the array definition above, *arr1* is holding seven characters. The total length of the string is six, the last index (sixth) is used for storing the terminating character.

```c
char arr2[9] = "STRING";
```

Data		S	T	R	I	N	G	'\0'		
Index		0	1	2	3	4	5	6	7	8

In the array definition above, *arr2* is capable of holding nine elements, but it is initialized to a string of six characters. The sixth index is occupied by a terminating character and the rest of the indices (seventh and eighth) are unused.

Accessing String Elements

String elements are accessed in a fashion similar to any other array. Array index and pointer arithmetic can be used to access the array elements.

Source code. String1.c

```c
#include <string.h>
int main(int argc, char* argv[])
{
        char* str = "Hello Pointer";
        int i = 0;
        for( i = 0; i< strlen(str); i++)
        {
                printf("%c",str[i]);
        }
        return 0;
}
```

In the code above, array indices are used to access the characters in a string. The function *strlen(char*)* is used to return the length of the string. This returned length does not account for the last null character that is always part of any string.

The code below uses a temporary character pointer variable *char* ptr* to traverse through the entire string. This example shows how a pointer can be used to access every character from the string.

Source code. String2.c

```c
#include <stdio.h>
int main(int argc, char* argv[])
{
        char* str = "Hello Pointer";
        char* ptr = str;
        while(*ptr != '\0')
        {
                printf("%c",*ptr);         //access characters
                ptr++;                     // traversing to next character position
        }
        return 0;
}
```

Dynamic Memory Allocation

The method of allocating dynamic memory to strings from the heap area is similar to that of any other array. Programmers should be careful while allocating the memory for a sequence of characters to be stored within an array for a string because an extra null character is required to terminate it at the end.

Source code. String3.c

```c
#include <string.h>
#include <malloc.h>
int main(int argc, char* argv[])
{
        char* src = "Hello Pointer";
        char* dst= NULL;
        dst = (char*)malloc(sizeof(char) * (strlen(src) + 1));
        memcpy(dst,src, strlen(src));
        return 0;
}
```

String Literals and Constants

When strings are defined, the compiler automatically concatenates an escape sequence of '\0' at the end of the string. String constants are also termed as string literals in some literature. A most interesting fact about string constants is that the memory is allocated to them from the RO section. The RO section is a read-only data area where string literals and constants are stored. The lifetime of the data stored in this section is throughout the lifecycle of the program execution and so is the life span of this variable too.

Source code. String4.c

```c
#include <stdio.h>
int* foo(void);
int main(int argc, char* argv[])
{
        int *m = foo();
        printf("Printing local value of function foo= %d\n", *m);
        return 0;
}
```

```
int* foo(void)
{
        int i = 10;
        return &i;
}
```

Output:

Printing local value of function foo = –858993460

In the code snippet above, the address of function foo() is stored in the variable *m* of the calling function main(). The calling function tries to print the value by dereferencing the pointer.

The output of the print statement is a garbage value because the pointer of the called function is pointing to a memory location that is not valid anymore. The memory area for variable *i* ceases to exist once the stack for the corresponding function goes out of life after the function call.

■ **Note**   In the program String1.c, it may happen that the *printf()* statement might print the value of 10 even though the memory region is not valid. Readers should try to reason this behavior.

Hint: *Look at the stack life cycle during program execution when a function call is made.*

Until now, you saw that once a function call is made and the control returns back to the callee function, the local variable of the called function cannot be accessed from the calling function. In the below code snippet, you will see an exception in this rule where it is possible to access the local variable from the calling function even after the function call is made.

Source code. String5.c

```
#include <stdio.h>
char* foo(void);
int main(int argc, char* argv[])
{
        char *m = foo();
        printf("Printing local value of function foo = %s\n", m);
        return 0;
}
char* foo(void)
{
        char* str = "STRING";
        return str;
}
```

Output:

Printing local value of function foo = STRING

Unlike the program String4.c, this program will always print the "STRING". Although the variable char* str is local to the function foo(), it is accessible within all scopes. As explained earlier, the variable char* str is a string literal or constant, and the memory is allocated from the RO section, which is persistent throughout the life cycle of program execution.

Another important characteristic of string literals is their nature of being constant. Once a string literal is initialized, its value cannot be changed at a later stage.

A string literal is equivalent to the const char* variable name, where a pointer can be modified but not the value that it is pointing to.

Source code. String6.c

```
#include <stdio.h>
int main()
{
        char *strliteral = "ADD";
        strliteral[0] = 'B';          //Modifying value of 0th index, NOT ALLOWED,
                                      //program will generate segmentation fault

        strliteral++ ; //Allowed
        return 0;
}
```

String Operations

As strings are capable of holding characters, there are a variety of operations that are performed on them. The common ones are as follows: string copy, string concatenation, string comparison, finding string length, etc. To get comfortable with these string operations, the next subsection elaborates on some basic implementations of these operations.

Handling String Inputs

As mentioned earlier, care should be taken to allocate enough memory area to store the characters in the string. Note that *"%s"* is the format used in the scanf() function to store the input string to a variable.

Source code. String7.c

```
#include <stdio.h>
#include <malloc.h>
int main()
{
        char arrstr[6];
        char* strptr;
        printf("Input hello\n");
        scanf(":%s", arrstr);
        strptr = (char*)malloc(sizeof(char)*10);
        printf("Input hello\n");
        scanf("%s", strptr);
}
```

String Iteration

Iterating over each and every index of any string variable is the most basic process that is performed to read or manipulate the data. The below code snippets explain how to read a string by reading each index one by one.

Source code. String8.c

```c
#include <stdio.h>
#include <malloc.h>
int main()
{
        char arrstr[6];
        char* strptr;
        printf("Input hello\n");
        scanf("%s", arrstr);
        printf("String received = %s\n",arrstr);
}
```

Source code. String9.c

```c
#include <stdio.h>
#include <malloc.h>
int main()
{
        char arrstr[6];
        char* strptr;
        printf("Input hello\n");
        scanf("%s", arrstr);
        strptr = arrstr;
        while(*strptr != '\0')
        {
                printf("%c",*strptr);
                strptr++;
        }
}
```

The code above shows how a variable char* strptr is initialized and points to the first location of the character array. The code loops until the value pointed to by the variable is not equal to the terminal character '\0'. Also, during each iteration, the variable is incremented to the next location with the help of pointer arithmetic *strptr++*.

String Length

String length by definition is the number of characters a string variable has stored. Since you know that string variables contain an extra terminating character, the net length of the string should only contain the sum of all the data in the strings and it should not add the count for the terminating character.

```c
int str_length(char* str)
{
        int string_length = 0;
        char* ptr = null;
        ptr = str;
        while(*ptr != '\0')
        {
                string_length++;
        }
        return string_length;
}
```

The code above iterates through the string until it reaches the terminating character '\0'. While iterating, it increments an integer variable to calculate the number of characters stored in that particular string.

String Copy

A string copy is an operation where data from one memory location pointed to by a string variable is copied to another memory location which is pointed to by another memory location.

Assuming that the dest_str variable has sufficient memory allocated for the new data that needs to be copied, the below code explains how a string can be copied to another memory location.

```
void str_copy(char* dest_str, const char* src_str)
{
        char* stemp = src_str;
        char* dtemp = dest_str;
        while(*stemp != '\0')
        {
                *dtemp = *stemp;
                stemp++;
                dtemp++;
        }
        *dtemp = '\0';
}
```

The code above iterates through the source string until it reaches the terminating character '\0'. While iterating, it copies every character to the destination string and it also increments the pointers for both the strings (source and destination). In the end, it copies the terminating character '\0' to the destination string.

String Concatenation

Concatenation of a string is an operation where a given string needs to be concatenated with another input string. Concatenation by default is implemented as concatenation at end. The code below explains how the concatenation can be implemented.

Source code. void str_cat(char* deststr, const char* srcstr)

```
{
        char* dtemp = deststr;
        char* stemp = srcstr;
        //reach till end of the deststr
        while(*dtemp != '\0')
        {
                dtemp++;
        }
        while(*srcstr != '\0')
        {
                *dtemp = *srcstr;
                dtemp ++;
                srcstr ++;
        }
        *dtemp = '\0';
}
```

The code above iterates through the destination string until it reaches the terminating character '\0'. Then, while iterating through the source string, it copies every character to the destination string and also increments the pointers for both the strings (source and destination). In the end, it copies the terminating character '\0' to the destination string.

Array of Strings

An array of strings contains pointers to arrays of characters or strings. Every string stored inside the array can be of different length. Figure 4-2 illustrates how an array of strings can be visualized. Each index contains a pointer to a string of variable length.

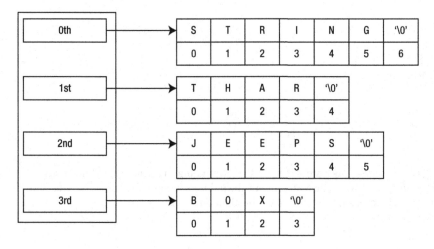

Figure 4-2. *Memory layout of array of strings*

Declaration of Array of Strings

A declaration of array of strings can be done in three ways. The declaration is governed by two important factors: first is the size of the array and second is the capacity of each index to hold the data. There are three ways to declare arrays of strings. The first two are using array notation and the last one is uses complete dynamic memory allocation. You will see all three of them with the help of examples. This section explains the array notation usage when size of the array and capacity of each index to hold the characters are known at compile time. To understand the memory layout and the declaration, an example of an array of strings declaration is used below. Let's assume that we have following declaration in the program:

```
char  str_arr[6][7];
```

In the above declaration of an array of strings, each row is capable of storing a string of up to six characters in length. The last index is used for storing the terminating character. Figure 4-3 explains the memory layout of the array of strings. You can see that all the indices are storing data of variable length. In this case, the length of string cannot be more than six since the last character will be the terminating character.

	0	1	2	3	4	5	6
0	E	G	R	E	T	'\0'	
1	I	B	I	S	'\0'		
2	M	Y	N	A	'\0'		
3	I	O	R	A	'\0'		
4	M	U	N	I	A	'\0'	
5	B	U	L	B	U	L	'\0'

Figure 4-3. *Memory layout of array of strings*

Source code. String10.c#include <stdio.h>

```c
int  main(int argc, char* argv[])
{
        char arr[6][10] = {
                "EGRET",
                "IBIS",
                "MYNA",
                "IORA",
                "MUNIA",
                "BULBUL"
        };
        int i;
        for(i = 0; i< 6; i++)
        {
                printf(" %d - %s\n", i, arr[i]);
        }
        return 0;
}
0 - EGRET
1 - IBIS
2 - MYNA
3 - IORA
4 - MUNIA
5 - BULBUL
```

The code above declares an array of strings that is capable of storing six strings whose maximum capacity to store characters is nine. The variable in the code snippets is initialized with the values. The for loop iterates over each index and prints the index and its corresponding string.

Now let's see how the array notation is used when size of array is not known and the capacity of each index to hold the characters is known at compile time. Let's assume that we have the following declaration in the program. In the method shown below, with the help of an array we have defined the number of pointers it can accommodate. But during runtime, each pointer is pointing to variable length strings. During iteration, each array index is made to point to dynamically allocated memory of variable length where the actual string will be stored.

char* str_arr2[10]; //An array of ten strings, where each character pointer at any particular index is capable of storing strings of varying lengths.

Source code. String11.c

```c
#include <stdio.h>
#include <string.h>
#include <malloc.h>
int main(int argc, char* argv[])
{
        char* arr[6];
        char tempstring[30];
        int i;
        for(i = 0 ; i< 6;i++)
        {
                printf("Insert data\n");
                scanf("%s",tempstring);
                arr[i] = (char*)malloc(sizeof(char)*(strlen(tempstring) + 1));
                strcpy(arr[i], tempstring);
        }
        printf("Data in array");
        for(i = 0; i< 6; i++)
        {
                printf(" %d - %s\n", i, arr[i]);
        }
        freestring(arr, 5);
                return 0;
}
freestring(char arr[], int length)
{
        int i;
        for( i = 0; i <= length; i++)
        {
                free(arr[i]);
        }
}

Insert data
EGRET
Insert data
IBIS
Insert data
MYNA
Insert data
IORA
Insert data
MUNIA
Insert data
BULBUL

    Data in array

0 - EGRET
1 - IBIS
2 - MYNA
```

```
3 - IORA
4 - MUNIA
5 - BULBUL
```

The freestring(char arr[], int length) method takes the address of a character array and its length. The code shown above has only assigned (dynamic allocation) space for the character strings during each iteration and it is pointed to by character pointers that are stored at each index of the array. So, in the freestring() method, every dynamically assigned memory is freed/deallocated during each iteration.

Now let's see the third way of declaring arrays of strings when size of array and capacity of each array index to hold the data is not known at compile time. This method of declaration is also known as a pointer-to-pointer declaration. Let's assume that we have the following declaration in the program:

```
char** dynamic_str;
```

Figure 4-4 illustrates the memory layout of the array of strings when pointer-to-pointer declaration is used. The reader can see that the data stored in the memory with respect to each index is of variable length.

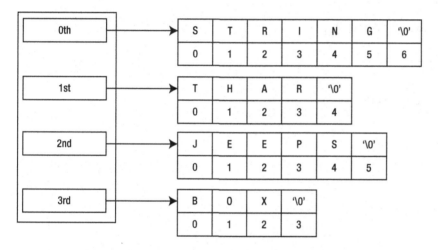

Figure 4-4. *Memory layout of a pointer-to-pointer declaration*

In the code below, we have used a different technique to store the array of strings. With the help of pointer to pointer to character, we have first created space to store the pointer, then for that pointer we have allocated space from the heap to store the string. From the second iteration onward, we have reallocated the memory to store the pointer and then allocated space from the heap to store the new string.

This method gives us an advantage over the two previous methods in such a way that not only can it store variable length strings, but also the number of pointers can be increased dynamically.

Source code. String12.c

```c
#include <stdio.h>
#include <string.h>
#include <malloc.h>
int main(int argc, char* argv[])
{
        char** arr = NULL;
        char tempstring[30];
```

```
        int i;
        for(i = 0 ; i< 6;i++)
        {
                printf("Insert data\n");
                scanf("%s",tempstring);
                if(arr == NULL)
                {
                        arr = (char**)malloc(sizeof(char*));
                }
                else
                {
                        arr = (char**)realloc(arr, sizeof(char*)*(i+1));
                }
                        arr[i] = (char*)malloc(sizeof(char)*(strlen(tempstring) + 1));
                        strcpy(arr[i], tempstring);
        }
        for(i = 0; i< 6; i++)
        {
                printf(" %d - %s\n", i, arr[i]);
        }
        freestrmemory(arr, 5);
        return 0;
}
void freestrmemory(char** arr, int length)
{
        int i;
        for( i = 0; i<=length; i++)
        {
                free(arr[i]);
        }
        free(arr);
}

Insert data
EGRET
Insert data
IBIS
Insert data
MYNA
Insert data
IORA
Insert data
MUNIA
Insert data
BULBUL

0 - EGRET
1 - IBIS
2 - MYNA
3 - IORA
4 - MUNIA
5 - BULBUL
```

Freeing memory in the above situation is a little tricky. Below are some basics steps that need to be followed to free the memory.

1. Iterate on each row of the array.

    a. While visiting each row, free the respective memory that is holding the string.

2. Once iterating through the array finishes, free the allocated memory that is holding all the pointers to the strings.

Figure 4-5 illustrates how the freeing steps take places. As explained above, first the iteration over the index takes place while iterating over each index we need to free the respective array. In the figure, this step is shown using a dashed line. After the completion of this step, the memory area of all the indices needs to be freed. And in the figure, this step is shown using the bold oval shape.

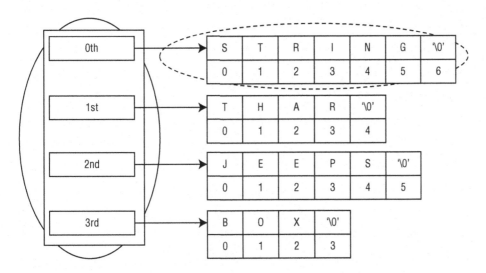

Figure 4-5. *Freeing steps in case pointer to pointer usage for array of strings*

Summary

In this chapter, we covered one of the most important aspects of pointers. There are many other string functions such as finding substrings, string reversal, trim at beginning, trim at end, etc. that were not covered in this chapter. Readers may try their hands on other library functions to gain command of manipulating strings.

Chapters 3 and 4 were focused on single-dimensional arrays and strings. In the next chapter, you will look into multi-dimensional arrays and learn how pointers help in manipulating them.

CHAPTER 5

■ ■ ■

Pointers and Multidimensional Arrays

Multidimensional arrays are one of the most important programming constructs in any programming language. From 2D, 3D, and onward, arrays are considered to be multidimensional. There are various syntaxes in C that are used to access multidimensional arrays. These syntaxes can sometimes take a very cryptic form and become difficult to understand. This chapter gives insight into the memory layout of multidimensional arrays and the ways the array indices are accessed with the help of pointers.

Before you start reading this chapter, you should keep in mind that some of the source code listed in this chapter outputs memory addresses. When you execute these programs on your device, the output with respect to the memory address may differ. The difference in output for memory address can be due to the use of different compilers and the underlying hardware. But you should not worry much about this difference because only the range of the addresses will change.

Array Layout

A 2D array can be visualized as a stack of 1D arrays, as shown in Figure 5-1. Each 1D row is laid out linearly in memory.

	COLUMNS			
	0	1	2	3
R O W S 0	0,0	0,1	0,2	0,3
1	1,0	1,1	1,2	1,3
2	2,0	2,1	2,2	2,3
3	3,0	3,1	3,2	3,3

Figure 5-1. A 2D array

As depicted above, the 0th row is laid out first, then the 1st row, and so on.

The source code below illustrates how a two-dimensional array is accessed. In the code, the expression *<variable_name>[row][column] (data[i][j])* is used.

Source code. MultiDim1.c

```
int main(int argc, char* argv[])
{
        int data[5][5];
        int i, j;
        for(i = 0; i<5;i++)
        {
                for(j = 0; j<5; j++)
                {
                        data[i][j] = -1;
                }
        }
        return 0;
}
```

Pointer to 2D Array

To understand the relation of pointers with multidimensional arrays, you need to get a clear understanding of array syntax and its meaning. Let's examine the meaning of following syntaxes.

Meaning of Syntax in a 1D Context

The following sections cover the syntax for a 1D array.

Specifying the Name of the Array Variable

Let's assume that we have a 1D array called int arr[10]; If we just specify the name of the array variable, it is equivalent to the address of 0th element.

arr = starting of the 0th element

Array Arithmetic

<Array variable name> + offset

This expression results in the address of the element that is at a distance of offset from the 0th element.

Accessing the Value at Location

To access the value at different locations or indexes, we use subscript notation. The use of subscripts, the meaning of syntax, and the value the expression yields slightly changes when it comes to multidimensional arrays. In this section, you will see methods of accessing the value at any particular location in a multidimensional array in detail.

To refresh the usage of subscript notation with a single dimension array, let's reiterate its concept. If arr[i] == i[arr] == *(arr+i), then we could access the ith element from the beginning of the array. All these expressions will yield the value at the ith index location of the array.

Meaning of Syntax in a 2D Context

The following sections cover the syntax for a 2D array.

Specifying the Name of the Array Variable

When the name of a variable is specified, it yields an address in the case of a 2D array. So, assuming *int arr[5][5]*, the variable named *arr* is just the name of an array variable. In case of a 2D array, specifying the name of an array will yield the address of the 0th row (which is a 1D array). And, adding an offset to the variable name will yield the starting address of the ith row. We can see the same result with the help of the following code snippet.

Source code. MultiDim2.c

```
#include <stdio.h>
int main(int argc, char* argv[])
{
        int data[5][5];
        int i, j;
        int count = 0;
        for(i = 0; i<5;i++)
        {
                for(j = 0; j<5; j++)
                {
                        data[i][j] = count++;
                }
        }
        printf("Starting address of the array %p\n", data);
        for(i = 0; i <5 ; i++)
        {
        printf(" %dth row location = %p\n", i, data[i]);
        printf("Loc %d,1 = %p\n", &data[i][0]);
        }
        return 0;
}
```

Output:
Starting address of the array 0046F904

```
0th row location = 0046F904
Loc 0,1 = 0046F904
1th row location = 0046F918
Loc 1,1 = 0046F918
2th row location = 0046F92C
Loc 2,1 = 0046F92C
3th row location = 0046F940
Loc 3,1 = 0046F940
4th row location = 0046F954
Loc 4,1 = 0046F954
```

In the code above, each row (which is itself a 1D array) is accessed with the help of a variable name and the 1st index (i.e., *data[i]*).

Therefore, the expression *<variable_name> + index == < variable_name >[index]* will yield the starting address of the ith row.

Example: *arr + i == arr[i]*

Arithmetic on an Address of an Array

For the expression *<variable name>[i] + offset*, we are adding the offset of the type that this object can hold. Since this is an integer array, four bytes are added to the base address of the array. Eventually, this will lead to the location of the second column in the same row. The code below illustrates how the above expression can be used to access each column of individual rows.

Source code. MultiDim3.c

```
#include <stdio.h>
int main(int argc, char* argv[])
{
        int data[5][5];
        int i, j;
        int count = 0;
        for(i = 0; i<5;i++)
        {
                for(j = 0; j<5; j++)
                {
                        data[i][j] = count++;
                }
        }
        for(i = 0; i<5;i++)
        {
                printf(" %d row = %p\n",i, data[i]);
                printf("Columns\n");
                for(j = 0; j<5; j++)
                {
                        printf("%d = %p, ",j, data[i] + j);
                }
                        printf("\n");
        }
        return 0;
}
```

   Output :

```
0 row = 002AFD08
Columns
0 = 002AFD08, 1 = 002AFD0C, 2 = 002AFD10, 3 = 002AFD14, 4 = 002AFD18,
1 row = 002AFD1C
Columns
0 = 002AFD1C, 1 = 002AFD20, 2 = 002AFD24, 3 = 002AFD28, 4 = 002AFD2C,
2 row = 002AFD30
Columns
0 = 002AFD30, 1 = 002AFD34, 2 = 002AFD38, 3 = 002AFD3C, 4 = 002AFD40,
3 row = 002AFD44
Columns
0 = 002AFD44, 1 = 002AFD48, 2 = 002AFD4C, 3 = 002AFD50, 4 = 002AFD54,
4 row = 002AFD58
Columns
0 = 002AFD58, 1 = 002AFD5C, 2 = 002AFD60, 3 = 002AFD64, 4 = 002AFD68,
```

Value at the Location

In a 2D array, to access the value at the ith row and j^{th} column, we specify it as follows:

```
<array var name>[row][column]
```

where row and column are indices.

For example: *arr[i][j];*
We can also specify it with pointer notation. Since we know that *arr[i] == Address of ith row*, if we add index *j* to this location, it will result in the jth column of this particular row *(arr[i] + j)*. So, the address of the *arr[i][j]* element can be obtained using *&arr[i][j]* or *(arr[i] + j)*.

To obtain the value of the ith row and j^{th} column, we can use the "value of" operator on both expressions above, as in **(&arr[i][j])* or **(arr[i] + j)*. Therefore we get *arr[i][j] == *(&arr[i][j])* or **(arr[i] + j) -- Expression 1.*

Also, in the context of a 1D array, the address of *arr[i] = &arr[i]* or *(arr + i)* value at the ith location can be obtained as follows:

```
arr[i] == *( &arr[i] ) == * ( arr + i ) -- Expression 2
```

So, from the Expression 2, we can substitute the value in Expression 1 and thus obtain

```
*( arr[ i] + j ) == *( *(arr + i ) + j )
```

There is a minor difference you need to understand about how the compiler interprets the expression while dealing with multidimensional arrays. In the case of a 1D array, **(arr + i)* will yield the value at the ith index while the same expression will yield the address of ith row in the case of 2D arrays.

As stated earlier, a 2D array is a stack of one-dimensional array of pointers; we can visualize it as follows:

	0	1	2	3
Address of 0th ROW				
	4	5	6	7
Address of 1st ROW				
	8	9	10	11
Address of 2nd ROW				
	12	13	14	15
Address of 3rd ROW				

We can use an array of pointers to access the array elements. Given *int arr[5][5];* we can write *int (*arrptr)[5] = arr;* The code below illustrates how to reach the base of the address of each single dimensional array.

Source code. MultiDim4.c

```c
#include <stdio.h>
int main(int argc, char* argv[])
{
        int data[5][5];
        int i, j;
```

```
        int count = 0;
        int (*aptr)[5];
        for(i = 0; i<5;i++)
        {
                for(j = 0; j<5; j++)
                {
                        data[i][j] = count++;
                }
        }
        aptr = data;
        for(i = 0; i <5 ; i++)
        {
                printf("%dth row = %p\n",i, *aptr++);
        }
        return 0;
}
```

Output:

```
0th row = 0036F74C
1th row = 0036F760
2th row = 0036F774
3th row = 0036F788
4th row = 0036F79C
```

*Note: *Under OS X (Xcode) on a Mac, the following results are returned:*

```
0th row = 0x7fff5fbff8e0
1th row = 0x7fff5fbff8f4
2th row = 0x7fff5fbff908
3th row = 0x7fff5fbff91c
4th row = 0x7fff5fbff930
```

In the code above, an array of pointers is used to point to the base address of each row (i.e., *aptr*).
The code below illustrates how the values of 2D array can be accessed with the array of pointer variables.

Source code. MultiDim5.c

```
#include <stdio.h>
int main(int argc, char* argv[])
{
        int data[5][5];
        int i, j;
        int count = 0;
        int (*aptr)[5];
        for(i = 0; i<5;i++)
```

```
        {
                for(j = 0; j<5; j++)
                {
                        data[i][j] = count++;
                }
        }
        aptr = data;
        for(i = 0; i <5 ; i++)
        {
                for(j = 0; j<5; j++)
                {
                        printf("%d,%d = %p val = %d \n",i, j, (*aptr + j), *(*aptr + j));
                }
                printf("\n");
                aptr++;
        }
        return 0;
}
```

Output:

```
0,0 = 0048FA94 val = 0
0,1 = 0048FA98 val = 1
0,2 = 0048FA9C val = 2
0,3 = 0048FAA0 val = 3
0,4 = 0048FAA4 val = 4
1,0 = 0048FAA8 val = 5
1,1 = 0048FAAC val = 6
.
.
```

In the code above, the array of pointers points to the base address of each row (i.e., *aptr*). Once the base address of a 1D array is reached, the second index can be used as an offset to access the individual elements of the array. So *(*aptr + j)* yields the address of the ith row and j[th] column. And **(*aptr + j)* yields a value at the address of the ith row and j[th] column.

Accessing the Indices with a Pointer Variable in the Case of 2D Array

The idea here is to access the 2D indices with the help of a pointer variable. This can be done in similarly to how the single dimension array is accessed with a pointer variable. To do so, we need to assign the address of the individual row to the pointer variable.

Source code. MultiDi6.c

```
#include <stdio.h>
int main(int argc, char* argv[])
{
        int data[5][5];
        int i, j;
```

```
        int count = 0;
        int (*aptr)[5];
        int *dataptr;
        for(i = 0; i<5;i++)
        {
                for(j = 0; j<5; j++)
                {
                        data[i][j] = count++;
                }
        }
        aptr = data;
        for(i = 0; i <5 ; i++)
        {
                printf("Address of %d row = %p\n", i,(*aptr + i));
                dataptr = (*aptr + i*5);
                for(j = 0; j<5; j++)
                {
                        printf("%d,%d = %p val = %d \n",i, j, dataptr, *(dataptr));
                        dataptr++;
                }
                printf("\n");
        }
        return 0;
}
```

In the code above, the address of each row is assigned to the integer pointer *int * dataptr*.

```
dataptr = (*aptr + i*5);
```

Then, the integer pointer is dereferenced to obtain the value at each index until the end of each row using *(dataptr)* and incrementing to reach the index of that row using *dataptr++.*

3D Array Layout

Similar to 2D array, a 3D array can be thought of or visualized as a stack of arrays, but with an exception that here each stack element is a 2D array.

```
                        ┌─────────────────────────────────┐
                        │           COLUMNS               │
                        └─────────────────────────────────┘

┌───┐   ┌───────────────────────────────────────────────────┐
│ R │   │ 0              Stack of 2D array                    │
│ O │   │   ┌───────────────────────────────────────────┐    │
│ W │   │   │ 0,0          Stack of 1D array              │    │
│ S │   │   │   ┌───────────────────────────────────┐    │    │
└───┘   │   │   │ 0,0,0    0,0,1     0,0,2    0,0,3  │    │    │
        │   │   └───────────────────────────────────┘    │    │
        │   │ 1,0                                         │    │
        │   │   ┌───────────────────────────────────┐    │    │
        │   │   │ 0,1,0    0,1,1     0,1,2    0,1,3  │    │    │
        │   │   └───────────────────────────────────┘    │    │
        │   │ 2,0                                         │    │
        │   │   ┌───────────────────────────────────┐    │    │
        │   │   │ 0,2,0    0,2,1     0,2,2    0,2,3  │    │    │
        │   │   └───────────────────────────────────┘    │    │
        │   └───────────────────────────────────────────┘    │
        │ 1                                                   │
        │   ┌───────────────────────────────────────────┐    │
        │   │ 0,0                                         │    │
        │   │   ┌───────────────────────────────────┐    │    │
        │   │   │ 1,0,0    1,0,1     1,0,2    1,0,3  │    │    │
        │   │   └───────────────────────────────────┘    │    │
        │   │ 1,0                                         │    │
        │   │   ┌───────────────────────────────────┐    │    │
        │   │   │ 1,1,0    1,1,1     1,1,2    1,1,3  │    │    │
        │   │   └───────────────────────────────────┘    │    │
        │   │ 2,0                                         │    │
        │   │   ┌───────────────────────────────────┐    │    │
        │   │   │ 1,2,0    1,2,1     1,2,2    1,2,3  │    │    │
        │   │   └───────────────────────────────────┘    │    │
        │   └───────────────────────────────────────────┘    │
        └───────────────────────────────────────────────────┘
```

In a linear view, 3D array is laid out as follows:

00 0	00 1	00 2	00 3	01 0	01 1	01 2	01 3	02 0	02 1	02 2	02 3	10 0	10 1	10 2	10 3

3D Array Basics

A 3D array is specified as follows with the help of three indices. Assuming that elements of the 3D array are integers and the dimensions are 5, 5, 5, we can define a variable as

```
int data[5][5][5];
```

The source code below illustrates how accessing of array elements in a 3D array is done.

Source code. MultiDim7.c

```c
#include <stdio.h>
int main(int argc, char* argv[])
{
        int data[3][3][3];
        int i, j, k;
        int count = 0;
        for(i = 0; i<3;i++)
        {
                for(j = 0; j<3; j++)
                {
                        for(k = 0; k <3; k++)
                        {
                                data[i][j][k] = count++;
                        }
                }
        }
        for(i = 0; i <3 ; i++)
        {
                for(j = 0; j<3; j++)
                {
                        for(k = 0; k <3; k++)
                        {
                                printf("%d%d%d= %d ",i,j,k,data[i][j][k]);
                        }
                        printf("\n");
                }
                printf("\n");
        }
        return 0;
}
```

   Output:

```
000= 0 001= 1 002= 2
010= 3 011= 4 012= 5
020= 6 021= 7 022= 8

100= 9 101= 10 102= 11
110= 12 111= 13 112= 14
120= 15 121= 16 122= 17
```

```
200= 18 201= 19 202= 20
210= 21 211= 22 212= 23
220= 24 221= 25 222= 26
```

Understanding 3D Array Expressions and their Meaning

The following sections cover 3D array expressions.

Specifying the Name of the Array Variable

Let's assume that we have a 3D array declared as *int data[5][5][5]*. The variable name of this array will yield the address of the 0th row. Since in the context of a 3D array every row contains a 2D array, this is also an address of the 0th row of a 1D array and an address of the 0th element of a 1D array (0, 0, 0).

Source code. MultiDim8.c

```c
#include <stdio.h>
int main(int argc, char* argv[])
{
        int data[3][3][3];
        int i, j, k;
        int count = 0;
        for(i = 0; i<3;i++)
        {
                for(j = 0; j<3; j++)
                {
                        for(k = 0; k <3; k++)
                        {
                                data[i][j][k] = count++;
                        }
                }
        }
        printf("0th row of 3d array = %p\n", data);
        printf("0th row of 2d array = %p\n", data[0][0]);
        printf("0th row of 1d array = %p\n", &data[0][0][0]);
        return 0;
}
```

Output:

```
0th row of 3d array = 0043F798
0th row of 2d array = 0043F798
0th row of 1d array = 0043F798

<variable_name> == address of the 0th row of 3D array

<variable_name>[0][0] == address of the 0th row of 2D array

&<variable_name>[0][0][0] = address of the 0th element of 1D array
```

Array Arithmetic

The expression below yields results of the address of the element whose location is at a distance of the offset from the 0th element.

```
<Array variable name> + offset
```

Keep in mind that there are three levels of indirection while working with a 3D array. At the first level, we see a 3D array as an array of 2D arrays So, if we add an offset at this level, it will add as many offsets as the size of the 2D arrays.

Source code. MultiDim9.c

```c
int main(int argc, char* argv[])
{
        int data[3][3][3];
        int i, j, k;
        int count = 0;
        for(i = 0; i<3;i++)
        {
                for(j = 0; j<3; j++)
                {
                        for(k = 0; k <3; k++)
                        {
                                data[i][j][k] = count++;
                        }
                }
        }
        for(i = 0; i<3;i++)
        {
                for(j = 0; j<3; j++)
                {
                        for(k = 0; k <3; k++)
                        {
                                printf("%d%d%d=%d addr %p ", i,j,k, data[i][j][k],&data[i][j][k]);
                        }
                        printf("\n");
                }
                printf("\n");
        }
        printf("Index value address\n");
        for(i = 0; i<3; i++)
        {
                printf("row %d addr = %p\n",i, data+i);
        }
        return 0;
}
```

Output:

Index value address

```
000=0 addr 003AF8BC 001=1 addr 003AF8C0 002=2 addr 003AF8C4
010=3 addr 003AF8C8 011=4 addr 003AF8CC 012=5 addr 003AF8D0
020=6 addr 003AF8D4 021=7 addr 003AF8D8 022=8 addr 003AF8DC

100=9 addr 003AF8E0 101=10 addr 003AF8E4 102=11 addr 003AF8E8
110=12 addr 003AF8EC 111=13 addr 003AF8F0 112=14 addr 003AF8F4
120=15 addr 003AF8F8 121=16 addr 003AF8FC 122=17 addr 003AF900

200=18 addr 003AF904 201=19 addr 003AF908 202=20 addr 003AF90C
210=21 addr 003AF910 211=22 addr 003AF914 212=23 addr 003AF918
220=24 addr 003AF91C 221=25 addr 003AF920 222=26 addr 003AF924

row 0 addr = 003AF8BC
row 1 addr = 003AF8E0
row 2 addr = 003AF904
```

As you can see in the output, the value of indices 0,0,0 - row 0 addr, 100 – row 1 addr, 200 – row 2 addr are the same. The expression $data[i] == data + i$ is equivalent and will lead us to an index of the ith row of the 2D array.

At the second level, we see a 2D array. Each 2D array is a stack of 1D arrays. We reach the second level by dereferencing the expression at level 1. Therefore, $*(data[i] + i) == data[i][j]$ is equivalent and will point to a 2D array. And also, $*data[i]$ will yield base address of the ith 2D array address of each element in the 3D array.

Source code. MultiDim10.c

```c
#include <stdio.h>
int main(int argc, char* argv[])
{
        int data[3][3][3];
        int i, j, k;
        int count = 0;
        for(i = 0; i<3;i++)
        {
                for(j = 0; j<3; j++)
                {
                        for(k = 0; k <3; k++)
                        {
                                data[i][j][k] = count++;
                        }
                }
        }
        for(i = 0; i<3;i++)
        {
                for(j = 0; j<3; j++)
                {
                        for(k = 0; k <3; k++)
                        {
                                printf("%d%d%d=%d addr %p ", i,j,k, data[i][j][k],&data[i][j][k]);
                        }
```

```
                        printf("\n");
                }
                printf("\n");
        }
        for(i = 0; i<3; i++)
        {
                printf("row %d addr = %p\n",i, data[0][i]);
        }
        printf("2D row address\n");
        for(i = 0; i<3; i++)
        {
                printf("3D %d ROW\n", i);
                for(j = 0; j<3; j++)
                {
                        printf("2D row %d addr = %p %p \n",j, data[i][j], *(data[i] + j));
                }
        }
        return 0;
}
```

Output:

```
000=0 addr 003BFCD0 001=1 addr 003BFCD4 002=2 addr 003BFCD8
010=3 addr 003BFCDC 011=4 addr 003BFCE0 012=5 addr 003BFCE4
020=6 addr 003BFCE8 021=7 addr 003BFCEC 022=8 addr 003BFCF0

100=9 addr 003BFCF4 101=10 addr 003BFCF8 102=11 addr 003BFCFC
110=12 addr 003BFD00 111=13 addr 003BFD04 112=14 addr 003BFD08
120=15 addr 003BFD0C 121=16 addr 003BFD10 122=17 addr 003BFD14

200=18 addr 003BFD18 201=19 addr 003BFD1C 202=20 addr 003BFD20
210=21 addr 003BFD24 211=22 addr 003BFD28 212=23 addr 003BFD2C
220=24 addr 003BFD30 221=25 addr 003BFD34 222=26 addr 003BFD38

row 0 addr = 003BFCD0
row 1 addr = 003BFCDC
row 2 addr = 003BFCE8

2D row address

3D 0 ROW

2D row 0 addr = 003BFCD0 003BFCD0
2D row 1 addr = 003BFCDC 003BFCDC
2D row 2 addr = 003BFCE8 003BFCE8

3D 1 ROW

2D row 0 addr = 003BFCF4 003BFCF4
2D row 1 addr = 003BFD00 003BFD00
2D row 2 addr = 003BFD0C 003BFD0C
```

3D 2 ROW

2D row 0 addr = 003BFD18 003BFD18
2D row 1 addr = 003BFD24 003BFD24
2D row 2 addr = 003BFD30 003BFD30

At the third level, we see 1D array and their values when we dereference it. We reach the first level by dereferencing the expression at level 2. Therefore, *(data[i] + i) + k) == data[i][j]+k* is equivalent and will point to the elements of a 1D array. And to get the element at these addresses, we need to use the "value of" operator.

```
*((*(data[i] + i) + k)) == *(data[i][j]+k) = d[i][j][k]
```

The code below illustrates the use of the expression above.

Source code. MultiDim11.c

```c
#include <stdio.h>
int main(int argc, char* argv[])
{
        int data[3][3][3];
        int i, j, k;
        int count = 0;
        for(i = 0; i<3;i++)
        {
                for(j = 0; j<3; j++)
                {
                        for(k = 0; k <3; k++)
                        {
                                data[i][j][k] = count++;
                        }
                }
        }
        printf("Index=val addr <>\n");
        for(i = 0; i<3;i++)
        {
                for(j = 0; j<3; j++)
                {
                        for(k = 0; k <3; k++)
                        {
                                printf("%d%d%d=%d addr %p ", i,j,k, data[i][j][k],&data[i][j][k]);
                        }
                        printf("\n");
                }
                printf("\n");
        }
        for(i = 0; i<3; i++)
        {
                printf("row %d addr = %p\n",i, data[0][i]);
        }
        printf("2D row address\n");
```

```
        for(i = 0; i<3; i++)
        {
                printf("3D %d ROW\n", i);
                for(j = 0; j<3; j++)
                {
                        printf("2D row %d addr = %p %p \n",j, data[i][j], *(data[i] + j));
                }
        }
        printf("1D element address\n");
        for(i = 0; i<3; i++)
        {
                printf("3D %d ROW\n", i);
                for(j = 0; j<3; j++)
                {
                        printf("2D %d row\n", j);
                        for(k = 0; k<3; k++)
                        {
                        printf("%d%d%d = %p val = %d ",i,j,k, *(data[i] + j) + k, *(*(data[i] + j) + k));
                        }
                        printf("\n");
                }
        }
        return 0;
}
```

Output:

```
Index=val addr <>

000=0 addr 0031FD24 001=1 addr 0031FD28 002=2 addr 0031FD2C
010=3 addr 0031FD30 011=4 addr 0031FD34 012=5 addr 0031FD38
020=6 addr 0031FD3C 021=7 addr 0031FD40 022=8 addr 0031FD44

100=9 addr 0031FD48 101=10 addr 0031FD4C 102=11 addr 0031FD50
110=12 addr 0031FD54 111=13 addr 0031FD58 112=14 addr 0031FD5C
120=15 addr 0031FD60 121=16 addr 0031FD64 122=17 addr 0031FD68

200=18 addr 0031FD6C 201=19 addr 0031FD70 202=20 addr 0031FD74
210=21 addr 0031FD78 211=22 addr 0031FD7C 212=23 addr 0031FD80
220=24 addr 0031FD84 221=25 addr 0031FD88 222=26 addr 0031FD8C

row 0 addr = 0031FD24
row 1 addr = 0031FD30
row 2 addr = 0031FD3C

2D row address

3D 0 ROW
```

```
2D row 0 addr = 0031FD24 0031FD24
2D row 1 addr = 0031FD30 0031FD30
2D row 2 addr = 0031FD3C 0031FD3C

3D 1 ROW

2D row 0 addr = 0031FD48 0031FD48
2D row 1 addr = 0031FD54 0031FD54
2D row 2 addr = 0031FD60 0031FD60

3D 2 ROW

2D row 0 addr = 0031FD6C 0031FD6C
2D row 1 addr = 0031FD78 0031FD78
2D row 2 addr = 0031FD84 0031FD84

1D element address

3D 0 ROW

2D 0 row
000 = 0031FD24 val = 0 001 = 0031FD28 val = 1 002 = 0031FD2C val = 2
2D 1 row
010 = 0031FD30 val = 3 011 = 0031FD34 val = 4 012 = 0031FD38 val = 5
2D 2 row
020 = 0031FD3C val = 6 021 = 0031FD40 val = 7 022 = 0031FD44 val = 8

3D 1 ROW

2D 0 row
100 = 0031FD48 val = 9 101 = 0031FD4C val = 10 102 = 0031FD50 val = 11
2D 1 row
110 = 0031FD54 val = 12 111 = 0031FD58 val = 13 112 = 0031FD5C val = 14
2D 2 row
120 = 0031FD60 val = 15 121 = 0031FD64 val = 16 122 = 0031FD68 val = 17

3D 2 ROW

2D 0 row
200 = 0031FD6C val = 18 201 = 0031FD70 val = 19 202 = 0031FD74 val = 20
2D 1 row
210 = 0031FD78 val = 21 211 = 0031FD7C val = 22 212 = 0031FD80 val = 23
2D 2 row
220 = 0031FD84 val = 24 221 = 0031FD88 val = 25 222 = 0031FD8C val = 26
```

Using a Pointer Variable to Access Each Element in a 3D Array

To access an individual array element, the same technique can be used as in the case of 2D array element access. The pointer variable must be pointing to the base address of the single dimension array that is part of every 2D array. In turn, this 2D array acts as an individual element of the 3D array as a whole. The code below illustrates how this can be realized.

Source code. MultiDim12.c

```c
#include <stdio.h>
int main(int argc, char* argv[])
{
        int data[3][3][3];
        int i, j, k;
        int count = 0;
        int *dataptr = NULL;
        for(i = 0; i<3;i++)
        {
                for(j = 0; j<3; j++)
                {
                        for(k = 0; k <3; k++)
                        {
                                data[i][j][k] = count++;
                        }
                }
        }
        for(i = 0; i<3; i++)
        {
                printf("3D %d ROW\n", i);
                for(j = 0; j<3; j++)
                {
                        printf("2D %d row\n", j);
                        dataptr = *(data[i]+j);
                        for(k = 0; k<3; k++)
                        {
                                printf("%d%d%d = %p val = %d ",i,j,k, dataptr, *dataptr++);
                        }
                        printf("\n");
                }
        }
        return 0;
}
```

In the code above, the expression *(data[i] + j) yields the ith 2D row, and in that 2D row it points to the base address of the jth 1D row. In the expression *dataptr = *(data[i]+j)* the pointer variable *dataptr* will be pointing to the 1D array, and we can access the value by dereferencing the same **dataptr*, and we can also iterate through the whole array by using the increment operation on the pointer variable (i.e., **dataptr++*).

Summary

Understanding and visualizing a 2D array as a stack of 1D arrays and a 3D array as stack of 2D arrays was the main highlight of this chapter. Also, emphasis was given on using pointers for referencing and dereferencing. This chapter also highlighted the meaning of cryptic syntaxes with respect to the pointers and 2D/3D arrays.

In the next chapter, you will see the details about the use of pointers with structures. Structures are the most fundamental part in creating specialized data structures, and pointers play important role in manipulating them.

CHAPTER 6

■ ■ ■

Pointers to Structures

A structure is a collection of variables within one variable. Structures can be termed as a variable that aggregates variables of different or similar types. The correlation of structures and pointers is very strong. A structure provides a very intuitive way to model user-defined entities (records, packet formats, image headers, etc.). This chapter explains the basics of structures and their use with pointers; it also explains how structures can be used to implement data structures like trees, linked lists, etc. in depth.

Defining Structures

The keyword in C that is used to define a structure is *struct*. Structures can contain variables of any kind that are permissible by the C language. They can also contain another structure variable within themselves. The following is an example of a typical way in which structures are defined:

```
struct variable_name
{
        variable_type1 variable_name1;
        variable_type2 variable_name2;
        variable_type3 variable_name3;
        •
        •
        //list could grow
}
```

Example:

```
struct header
{
        int  header_version;
        char tagid;
        char signature[4];
        int data_offset;
}
```

Declaring Structure Variables

Structure variables are declared similarly to other variables in C, but it is usually a two-step process.

1. Define the structure.

2. Declare the variables of the respective structure type.

```
//Defining a structure below

struct date
{
        int day;
        int month;
        int year;
};
struct date currentdate; // Declaring the variable "currentdate" which is of type struct date
```

Accessing Structure Members

Member fields of a structure variable are accessed using a dot (.) operator. The syntax for accessing them is as follows:

```
<variable_name> . <memberfieldname>
```

The source code below illustrates an example of how structure member fields are accessed using a dot operator.

Source code. Struct1.c

```
int main(int argc, char* argv[])
{
        struct date
        {
                int day;
                int month;
                int year;
        };
        struct date current;
        current.day = 1;
        current.month = 11;
        current.year = 2012;
        return 0;
}
```

Initializing Structure Variables

There are two methods to initialize structure variables.

Method 1

After declaring a structure variable, each member is initialized individually. The dot operator is used to access the member variables. Refer to the code above in struct1.c to see how the variable *struct data current* is initialized after its declaration.

Method 2

Structure variables can be initialized with the use of set notation. In set notation, the values are written in ordered form with a comma separating the opening and closed curly braces. The member fields get initialized with the values found in the specified order. The code below illustrates this method of initializing the structure member fields.

Source code. Struct2.c

```
int main(int argc, char* argv[])
{
        struct date
        {
                int day;
                int month;
                int year;
        };
        struct date current = { 1, 11,  2012 };
        return 0;
}
```

Structure Nesting

The code above shows how a structure aggregates other data types. It is also possible to embed structure variables within a structure. This nesting can go up to many levels, as shown in the definition below.

```
struct header
{
        int version;
        int signature;
        struct tagname
        {
                int id;
                int offset;
        }tagid;
};
```

The nested structure variable is accessed similarly to other variables in the structure (i.e., using a variable name).

Source code. Struct3.c

```
int main(int argc, char * argv[])
{
        struct header
        {
                int version;
                int signature;
```

```
                    //below is structure variable definition and declaration

                    struct tagname
                    {
                            int id;
                            int offset;
                    } tagid;
          };

      struct header hdrinfo;
      hdrinfo.version = 0;
      hdrinfo.signature = 5;
      hdrinfo.tagid.id = 1;        //accessing embedded variables through variable name
      hdrinfo.tagid.offset = 10; //accessing embedded variables through variable name
      return 0;
}
```

Structure in Memory

A structure data type variable is very similar to an array when loaded in memory. All the member fields take consecutive memory locations.

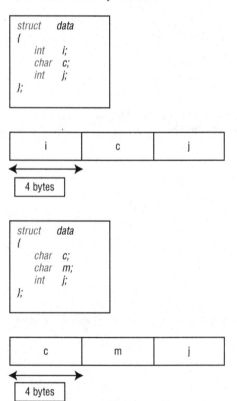

The size of a structure variable is equivalent to the total size of all the variables it contains. Assuming a *char* takes one byte and an integer takes four bytes, let's analyze the size of structure variables.

Source code. Struct4.c

```
int main(int argc, char * argv[])
{
        struct data
        {
                int i;
                int j;
                int k;
        };

        struct data v1;
        printf("Size of structure data = %d\n", sizeof(struct data));
        return 0;
}
```

Output:

```
Size of structure data = 12
```

You can see in the code snippet above that the output size of the *struct data* is 12 bytes because it contains three integer variables (*i, j, k*).

Structure Padding

Structure padding is the step taken by the compiler to align the data at a memory offset. First, we will take a look at alignment and then we will see how this is accomplished through structure padding.

Data Alignment

When a CPU reads or writes into memory, it does the job in small chunks (called word size or 4 bytes). This arrangement increases the performance of the system. Effectively, it puts the data at the offset/address that is a multiple of a word size. Imagine a processor that reads/writes in word size units.

In Figure 6-1, let's assume that the job of the processor is to read four words from the memory and place them in registers. This is the ideal condition since the offsets are at multiples of a word size (0, 1, 2). The processor will take one cycle for fetching a word.

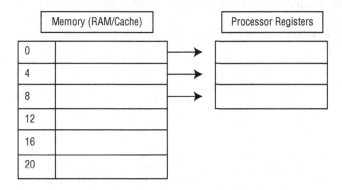

Figure 6-1. *Reading data from RAM/cache*

Imagine a case where the data is not stored at the offsets that are multiples of word size. In Figure 6-2, we can see a situation where data of size word is stored from location 2nd – 3rd – 4th – $5^{th.}$ Here, we are assuming that the 0th and 1st locations are either empty or some data is already stored there.

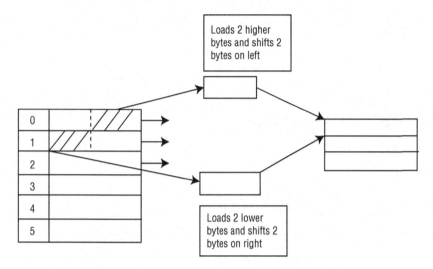

Figure 6-2. *Alignment process*

First, the processor will load one word from the 0th location and shifts two bytes to the left to get the most significant two bytes. Then it fetches another word from the 1st location and shifts two bytes to the right to get the least significant two bytes. After doing so, it will merge both the results to get the final word.

Eventually, the processor takes two cycles to fetch one word when the desired data is misaligned. The extra cycle has a drastic impact on the performance of the code. There are situations where some processors generate an alignment exception and it tends to slow down the fetching process even more.

Effectively, different data types need to be naturally aligned as per their sizes. One byte is aligned for a *char* (also char in assembly language), two bytes aligned for a *short int* (word in assembly language), four bytes aligned for an *int* (dword in assembly language), eight bytes aligned for a *double* (qword in assembly language), and so on.

Structure Padding

As explained above, for performance, the compiler tries to address the data alignment in the structure with a method called structure padding.

Suppose we have linear memory and each slot is capable of holding data of word size. Let's review the memory mapping of different structures when loaded in this linear memory.

Case 1

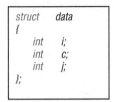

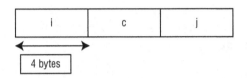

In the situation above, you can see that each of the member variables (*int i, int c, int j*) fits perfectly in each slot of the memory because the size of the data type is the same (a word). This situation is perfectly fine with respect to data alignment as all the data members are placed at the offset multiples of a word size.

Case 2

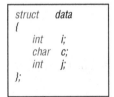

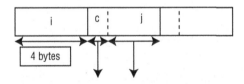

The structure above, *struct data* has three members (*int i, char c,* and *int j*). When the structure gets loaded in memory, *int i* starts at an offset of the 0th byte, *char c* starts at an offset of the 5th byte, and *int j* starts at an offset of the 6th byte. With the arrangement above, you can see that when the process tries to access the variable *j*, it will take two cycles to do so because *int j* is not aligned to the offset which is a multiple of the word size.

To rectify this issue, the compiler adds the required number of bytes to align the members of the data structure when required. As mentioned before, this action of adding bytes to align the member fields is termed structure padding.

Structure padding can be verified with the help of a *sizeof()* function. In the structure above, *struct data*, we would expect that the size of this structure variable will be a sum of all the data members it contains.

```
SIZEOF int j + SIZEOF char c + SIZEOF int j = 4 bytes + 1 byte + 4 bytes = 9 bytes
```

However, the program below reveals that the size of the variable is 12 bytes. Also, the address of each data member reveals that extra bytes have been padded after the data member *char c*.

Source code. Struct 5.c

```
#include <stdio.h>
int main(int argc, char* argv[])
{
        struct data
        {
                int i;
                char c;
                int j;
        };
        struct data v1;
        struct data *dsptr;
        printf("Size of structure data = %d\n", sizeof(struct data));
        dsptr = (struct data*)malloc(sizeof(struct data));
        printf("Address of member int i = %u\n", &(dsptr->i));
        printf("Address of member char c = %u\n", &(dsptr->c));
        printf("Address of member int j = %u\n", &(dsptr->j));
        return 0;
}
```

Output:

```
Size of structure data = 12
Address of member int i = 1263240
Address of member char c = 1263244
Address of member int j = 1263248
```

You can clearly see that the member *int j* is starting from an offset that is four bytes after the offset of the member *char c.*

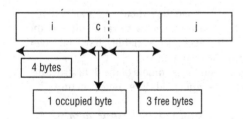

Source code. Struct 6.c

```c
#include <malloc.h>
int main(int argc, char* argv[])
{
        struct data
        {
                int i;
                char c1;
                int j;
                char c2;
                int k;
        };
        struct data v1;
        struct data *dsptr;
        printf("Size of structure data = %d\n", sizeof(struct data));
        dsptr = (struct data*)malloc(sizeof(struct data));
        printf("Address of member int i = %u\n", &(dsptr->i));
        printf("Address of member char c1 = %u\n", &(dsptr->c1));
        printf("Address of member int j = %u\n", &(dsptr->j));
        printf("Address of member char c2 = %u\n", &(dsptr->c2));
        printf("Address of member int k = %u\n", &(dsptr->k));
        return 0;
}
```

Output:

```
Size of structure data = 20
Address of member int i = 2377352
Address of member char c1 = 2377356
Address of member int j = 2377360
Address of member char c2 = 2377364
Address of member int k = 2377368
```

In the program above, there are two holes (one after variable *char c1* and another after variable *char c2*). You can clearly see that the compiler has done the structure padding for those two variables.

Xcode returns the following addresses for a Mac computer:

```
Size of structure data = 20
Address of member int i = 1063424
Address of member char c1 = 1063428
Address of member int j = 1063432
Address of member char c2 = 1063436
Address of member int k = 1063440
```

When Structure Padding is not Helpful

Data structures are very commonly used with images, packets, etc. Basically, a file or a packet is read into a buffer, and to access the header information or the fields, they are type casted to a proper structure.

Let's write a structure based on the hypothetical GIF image based on the information in Table 6-1.

Table 6-1. *GIF Header Format*

Offset	Size	Description
0	3 bytes	Signature
3	3 bytes	Version
6	4 bytes	Width
10	4 bytes	Height
14	1 byte	Colormap
15	1 byte	Bgcolor
16	1 byte	Ratio

```
struct gif_hdr
{
        char signature[3];
        char version[3];
        int width;
        int height;
        char colormap;
        char bgcolor;
        char ratio;
};
```

```
0 1 2 3 4 5 6        10       14    15      16

┌───────┬───────┬───────┬───────┬────┬────┬────┬──────────────┐
│   3   │   3   │   4   │   4   │ 1  │ 1  │ 1  │  Image data  │
└───────┴───────┴───────┴───────┴────┴────┴────┴──────────────┘

┌───────────────────────────────────────────────────────────┐
│                       Image data                           │
└───────────────────────────────────────────────────────────┘
```

Assume that we have a jpeg file with a jpeg header at the beginning of the file followed by the image data. Usually, we read the file into a buffer and type cast it with the appropriate structure to decode the header.

Notice that the size of the jpeg header is 3+3+4+4+1+1+1 = 17 bytes

   1st member is located at the 0th location

   2nd member is located at the 3rd location

   3rd member is located at the 6th location

   4th member is at the 10th location

   5th member is at the 14th location

   6th member is at the 15th location

   7th member is at the 16th location

The source code below illustrates the concept of data alignment. With the help of offsets, you can understand how the data is placed in the memory.

Source code. Struct 7.c

```
int main(int argc, char* argv[])
{
        struct gif_hdr
        {
                char signature[3];
                char version[3];
                int width;
                int height;
                char colormap;
                char bgcolor;
                char ratio;
        };
        struct gif_hdr v1;
        struct gif_hdr *dsptr;
        printf("Size of structure data = %d\n", sizeof(struct gif_hdr));
        dsptr = (struct gif_hdr*)malloc(sizeof(struct gif_hdr));
        printf("Offset of signature = %d\n", &(dsptr->signature[0]) - &(dsptr->signature[0]) );
        printf("Offset of version = %d\n", &(dsptr->version[0]) - &(dsptr->signature[0]) );
        printf("Offset of width = %d\n", (char*)&(dsptr->width) - &(dsptr->signature[0]));
        printf("Offset of height = %d\n", (char*)&(dsptr->height) - &(dsptr->signature[0]));
        printf("Offset of colormap = %d\n", &(dsptr->colormap) - &(dsptr->signature[0]));
        printf("Offset of bgcolor = %d\n",&(dsptr->bgcolor) - &(dsptr->signature[0]));
        printf("Offset of ratio = %d\n", &(dsptr->ratio) - &(dsptr->signature[0]));
        return 0;
}
```

Output:

```
Size of structure data = 20
Offset of signature = 0
Offset of version = 3
Offset of width = 8
Offset of height = 12
Offset of colormap = 16
Offset of bgcolor = 17
Offset of ratio = 18
```

After considering the header format earlier, we calculated the size of the gif header as 17 bytes. But, the program states the size of the structure as 20 bytes. This implicitly means that the compiler has performed structure padding at the required places.

As per the analysis, the required offset of header fields will be at the following offsets:

0 3 6 10 14 15 16

However, according to the output of the program, the offsets of the structure members are at the following places:

0 3 8 12 16 17 18

If we open a GIF file in a program for decoding and typecast our structure *struct gif_hdr* and then we try to access the member fields, we will be accessing the values at the wrong offsets because they are already misaligned due to padded bytes/bits.

So, when you are working with image headers, binary headers, and network packets, and are trying to access the TCP/ IP header, structure padding has to be avoided.

Structure Packing

To avoid structure padding, you can use #pragma directives or you can use a "packed" directive in the case of the GNU C compiler.

The PRAGMA directive can be used as follows:

```
#pragma pack ( 1 ) // 1 - byte alignment
struct data
{
        int I ;
        char c;
        int j;
};
```

A packed directive can be used in two ways.

1. Directly against the members of structure.

```
struct data
{
        int i __attribute__((__packed__));
        char c __attribute__((__packed__));
        int k __attribute__((__packed__));
};
```

2. Against the complete structure.

```
struct data
{
        int i ;
        char c ;
        int k;
} __attribute__((__packed__));
```

Using the earlier example of the gif header, let's modify the structure and see how a packed structure can help in accessing the correct offsets.

Source code. Struct 8.c

```
int main(int argc, char* argv[])
{
        struct gif_hdr
        {
                char signature[3];
                char version[3];
```

```
            int width;
            int height;
            char colormap;
            char bgcolor;
            char ratio;
      };
      struct gif_hdr v1;
      struct gif_hdr *dsptr;
      printf("Size of structure data = %d\n", sizeof(struct gif_hdr));
      dsptr = (struct gif_hdr*)malloc(sizeof(struct gif_hdr));
      printf("Offset of signature = %d\n", &(dsptr->signature[0]) - &(dsptr->signature[0]) );
      printf("Offset of version = %d\n", &(dsptr->version[0]) - &(dsptr->signature[0]) );
      printf("Offset of width = %d\n", (char*)&(dsptr->width) - &(dsptr->signature[0]));
      printf("Offset of height = %d\n", (char*)&(dsptr->height) - &(dsptr->signature[0]));
      printf("Offset of colormap = %d\n", &(dsptr->colormap) - &(dsptr->signature[0]));
      printf("Offset of bgcolor = %d\n",&(dsptr->bgcolor) - &(dsptr->signature[0]));
      printf("Offset of ratio = %d\n", &(dsptr->ratio) - &(dsptr->signature[0]));
      return 0;
}
```

Output:

```
Size of structure data = 20
Offset of signature = 0
Offset of version = 3
Offset of width = 6
Offset of height = 10
Offset of colormap = 14
Offset of bgcolor = 15
Offset of ratio = 16
```

Looking at the output above, we can see that we have the desired offsets for the member field as the gif header has prescribed.

Structure Assignment and Copying

Assigning a structure variable to another works like normal assignments. The respective values for member variables are copied from one structure to another.

Source code. Struct 9.c

```
#include <malloc.h>
int main(int argc, char* argv[])
{
      struct data
      {
            int i;
            char c;
            int j;
            int arr[2];
      };
```

```
        struct datawptr
        {
                int i;
                char *c;
        };
        struct datawptr dptr1;
        struct datawptr dptr2;
        struct data svar1;   // a normal variable of type struct data
        struct data svar2;   // a normal variable of type struct data
        svar1.c = 'a';
        svar1.i = 1;
        svar1.j = 2;
        svar1.arr[0] = 10;
        svar1.arr[1] = 20;
        svar2 = svar1;
        printf("Value of second variable \n");
        printf("Member c = %c\n", svar2.c);
        printf("Member i = %d\n", svar2.i);
        printf("Member j = %d\n", svar2.j);
        printf("Member arr0th = %d\n", svar2.arr[0]);
        printf("Member arr1st = %d\n", svar2.arr[1]);
        dptr1.i = 10;
        dptr1.c = (char*)malloc(sizeof(char));
        *(dptr1.c) = 'c';
        dptr2.c = (char*)malloc(sizeof(char));
        dptr2 = dptr1;
        printf("int member = %d\n", dptr2.i);
        printf("char ptr member = %c\n", *(dptr2.c));
        return 0;
}
```

Output:

```
Value of second variable
Member c = a
Member i = 1
Member j = 2
Member arr0th = 10
Member arr1st = 20
int member of dptr2 = 10
char ptr member of dptr2 = c
```

All the member fields get copied to the respective member's of the assigned structure variable.

The *memcpy()* function from the library will also have the same effect as an assignment operator. But, with the above approach, one needs to be careful when a data structure contains a member of pointer type because the assignment operator simply copies the value; it will also copy the pointer variable's value, which is nothing but the address of some variable it is pointing to. Later, when the assigned variable tries to change the value at that address, it eventually changes the value in the source variable's address.

Source code. Struct 10.c

```
int main(int argc, char* argv[])
{
        struct datawptr
        {
                int i;
                char *c;
        };
        struct datawptr dptr1;
        struct datawptr dptr2;
        dptr1.i = 10;
        dptr1.c = (char*)malloc(sizeof(char));
        *(dptr1.c) = 'c';
        dptr2.c = (char*)malloc(sizeof(char));
        memcpy(&dptr2, &dptr1, sizeof(struct datawptr));
        printf("Int member value of 2nd variable = %d\n", dptr2.i);
        printf("Char ptr member value of 2nd variable = %c\n", *(dptr2.c));
        printf("value of char ptr in 1st variable = %p\n", dptr1.c);
        printf("value of char ptr in 2nd variable = %p\n", dptr2.c);
        printf("Changing value of 2nd member in 2nd variable (dptr2)\n");
        *(dptr2.c) = 'a';
printf("value of char ptr of 2nd variable = %c and 1st variable = %c\n", *(dptr2.c),
*(dptr1.c));
        return 0;
}
```

Output:

```
Int member value of 2nd variable = 10
Char ptr member value of 2nd variable = c
value of char ptr in 1st variable = 000C6A18
value of char ptr in 2nd variable = 000C6A18
Changing value of 2nd member in 2nd variable (dptr2)
value of char ptr of 2nd variable = a and 1st variable = a
```

Also, in the situation above, if we try to free the memory separately for the two variables, it will generate segfault (segmentation fault) because the first call for free via the 1st variable will free the memory once, and the second call for free via the 2nd variable will lead to a segfault as it is trying to free the same memory location for the second time.

Structure Pointers

A structure pointer variable is declared similarly to any other pointer variable.

```
struct <struct name > *<variable name>;
```

Example:

```
struct data
{
        int i;
        char c;
        int k;
};
struct data *var; // declaring a pointer variable " var" of type struct data
```

Accessing Member Variables

There are two operators that are used to access the member of structure data type with the help of structure pointer. We are assuming here that *variable_name* is a pointer variable of some *struct* data type

Dot Operator (.) Method

In this method, the dot operator is used to access the individual member fields of structure variables.

```
 ( * variable_name ) .member_field_name ;
(* var ) . c;
```

Since we are accessing the member field through a pointer variable, first we need to dereference the variable and then we need to access the member field with the help of the dot operator.

Be careful while using the method mentioned above to access the member variables. The dot operator [.] has a higher precedence over the "value at" operator [*]. If we analyze the precedence for instruction without brackets, it will be interpreted in the following way:

```
*var . c
```

In the C statement below, the compiler will interpret the code with the dot operator because of higher precedence, and eventually the instruction will be trying to access a pointer variable as a value, which is wrong.

```
* ( var .c  );
```

Arrow Operator (->) Method

In this method, the arrow operator is used to access the individual member fields of structure variables.

```
variable_name -> member_field_name
var -> c;
```

The source code below illustrates the usage of both the above explained methods.

Source code. Struct 11.c

```
#include <stdio.h>
int main(int argc, char* argv[])
{
        struct data
```

```
        {
                int i;
                char c;
                int j;
        };
        struct data *sptr; //pointer variable of type struct data
        struct data svar;  // a normal variable of type struct data
        sptr = (struct data*) malloc (sizeof(struct data)); //the code below is accessing the member
fields with help of arrow operator ->
        sptr->c = 'c';
        sptr->i = 10;
        sptr->j = 20;     //or the same variable could be access in the following way
        (*sptr).c = 'd';
        (*sptr).i = 30;
        (*sptr).j = 40;  //below code is accessing the member fields with help of dot operator
svar.c = 'a';
        var.i = 1;
        svar.j = 2;       //or the same variable could be access in the following way, using address
                          // of operator and arrow operator
        (&svar)->c = 'c';
        (&svar)->i = 3;
        (&svar)->j = 4;
        return 0;
}
```

Passing Structure Pointer Variable

A structure pointer variable is passed to a function like any other normal parameter. Passing a structure pointer has an advantage over passing the value. As stated earlier, when a pointer variable is passed, and if the value is modified, the update is effective in the scope of the caller. Let's assume that we have a very big structure variable with more than 15 data members. If we pass by value to send this variable to a function, it will take more time as compared to pass by address (in this case we will use a pointer variable).

Source code. Struct 12.c

```
struct node
{
        int data;
        char c;
};

int main()
{
        struct node v1;
        struct node* p1 = &v1;
        foo_passbyvalue( v1);
        foo_passbyaddr( p1 );
}

void foo_passbyvalue(struct node v)
{
        //do something
}
```

```
void foo_passbyaddr(struct node* p)
{
        //do something
}
```

The code above illustrates two functions:

a.   foo_passbyvalue(struct node)

This function is used to pass the structure variable with the help of the "pass by value" technique.

b.   foo_passbyaddr(struct node *)

This function is used to pass the structure variable with the help of the "pass by address" technique.

Common Mistakes

Many programmers try to assign the pointer as shown in the below program, thinking that by passing the pointer variable to a function and modifying it, it will be effective in the caller function. But, in the above scenario, we are passing the value of pointer variable. So, effectively after the function call *addnode()*, variable *n1* is still pointing to NULL.

Source code. Struct 13.c

```
struct node{
        int data;
};

void addnode(struct node* n1)
{
        n1 = (struct node*)malloc(sizeof(struct node));
        n1->data = 9;
}

int main(int argc, char* argv[])
{
        struct node* n1 = NULL;
        addnode(n1);
        return 0;
}
```

To rectify this, we need to pass the address of the pointer variable as shown in the program below.

Source code. Struct 14.c

```
struct node
{
        int data;
};

void addnode(struct node** n1)
{
        *n1 = (struct node*)malloc(sizeof(struct node));
        (*n1)->data = 9;
}
```

```
int main(int argc, char* argv[])
{
        struct node* n1 = NULL;
        addnode(&n1);
        return 0;
}
```

Type Casting Structure Pointers

Type casting is another aspect of programming used commonly with structure pointers. Type casting is a way of converting a variable of one data type to a variable of another data type. The source code below illustrates an example where typecasting is done on different structure variables.

Source code. Struct 15.c

```
int main()
{
        struct signature
        {
                char sign;
                char version;
        };
        struct id
        {
                char id;
                char platform;
        };
        struct data
        {
                struct signature sig;
                struct id idv;
                char data[100];
        };
        struct data* img;
        receivedata(img);
        struct signature* sign = extractsignature( &img);
        struct id* idval = extractid( &img);
}

struct signature* extractsignature(struct data* d)
{
        struct signature* sig = (struct signature*)d;
        return sig;
}

struct id* extracted( struct data* d)
{
        struct id* idv = (struct id*)d;
        return idv;
}
```

Self-Referential Structures

Structures can have pointer variables as their member fields. Specifically, we can declare a member field that is a pointer variable of type that is the same as the structure that is containing it.

Example:

```
struct node
{
        int data;
        struct node* self;
}
```

Self-referential structures form the building blocks of many complex data structures (linked lists, trees, graphs, etc.)

Data Structures and Algorithms

Structure data types are the building blocks of various data types that are very fundamental to computer science. This section gives an overview of such data structures (linked lists, trees, etc.).

Linked Lists

You can imagine a linked list as a chain of objects where each object is pointing to the next with a special rule for the first and last object. The first object is always pointed to by the root object and the last object will always point to some special value (NULL) to mark the end of the list/chain. A list of this kind is always accessed via the special object root.

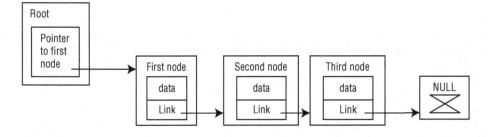

Linked list creation can be performed as follows:

1. Add a node at the beginning.

2. Add a node at the end.

3. Sorted insertion.

Other operations performed on linked list are as follows:

1. Searching the linked list.

2. Deleting a node from the linked list.

3. Counting nodes in a linked list.

The code below illustrates how a linked list is formed with the function *addatend(struct node** root, struct node* n)*. A helper function *createnode(int data)* is used. It takes the data and returns a new node with the data part copied and the next link set to NULL. This new node is passed to the *addatend()* function. In the *adddatend()* function, the first node (i.e. root) is checked if it is NULL. If it is NULL, then the new node is attached to the root, or else the code iterates to the last node by searching for the NULL node and there it adds the new node.

Source code. Struct 16.c

```
#include <malloc.h>
#include <stdio.h>

struct node
{
        int data;
        struct node* next;
};
struct node* createnode(int data)
{
        struct node* n1 = (struct node*)malloc(sizeof(struct node));
        n1->data = data;
        n1->next = NULL;
        return n1;
}
void addatend(struct node** root, struct node* n)
{
        struct node* temp = *root;
        if(temp == NULL)
        {
                *root = n;
        }
        else
        {
                while(temp->next != NULL)
                        temp = temp->next;
                temp->next = n;
        }
}
int main(int argc, char* argv[])
{
        struct node* root = NULL;
        for(int i = 0; i< 10;i++)
        {
                addatend(&root, createnode(i));
        }
        return 0;
}
```

Binary Search Tree

A binary search tree, illustrated in Figure 6-3, is constructed in such a way that at any level, the value stored by the immediate left node of any node is always lesser or equal to the value stored by itself. Thus, the left subtree of a node always contains the nodes storing the values less than or equal to the value stored in it. Similarly, the right subtree of a node always contains the nodes storing the values greater than or equal to the values stored in it.

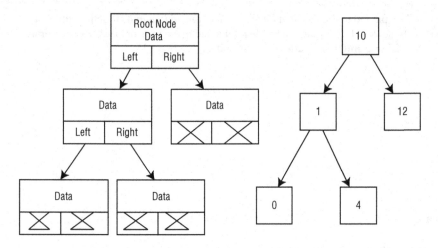

Figure 6-3. *Binary search tree*

Data structure for binary search tree (BST):

```
struct node
{
        int data;
        struct node* left;
        struct node* right;
};
```

Usually, we have data fields where any information on each node can be kept. The other two most important fields are left and right child pointers. These two variables help in forming the actual tree.

Creation of a BST

The code below illustrates how a BST can be created.

Source code. Struct 17.c

```
#include <string.h>
#include <malloc.h>
#include <stdio.h>

struct node
{
        int data;
        struct node* left;
        struct node* right;
};
struct node* createnode(int data)
{
        struct node* n1 = (struct node*)malloc(sizeof(struct node));
                n1->data = data;
        n1->left = NULL;
```

```
            n1->right = NULL;
            return n1;
}
void insertnode(struct node** root, struct node* n)
{
            struct node* temp = *root;
            if(temp == NULL)
            {
                    *root = n;
            }
            else
            {
                    if(n->data < temp->data)
                    {
                            insertnode(&(temp->left), n);
                    }
                    else if( n->data > temp->data)
                            {
                                    insertnode(&(temp->right), n);
                            }
            }
}
int main(int argc, char* argv[])
{
            struct node* root = NULL;
            for(int i = 0;  i< 10;i++)
            {
                    insertnode(&root, createnode(i));
            }
            return 0;
}
```

The code above starts at the root node and compares the data part of the current node it has visited with the new node that is going to be inserted. If the value of the new node's data is less than the current node's data, it recursively calls the same function by passing a pointer of the left child; otherwise, it recursively calls the same function by passing the pointer of the right child.

Iterating Over the Nodes

The following are the algorithms used to iterate over the nodes in BST:

1.   In order search

2.   Preorder search

3.   Post order search

Other helper functions that can be written for BST are as follows:

- Finding the height of the tree.

- Comparing the two BSTs.

- Finding the number of leaf nodes, and so on.

Summary

This chapter focused on the memory layout of structure variables and many other details like alignment issues, padding concepts, etc. With that background, the chapter introduced the concept of pointers to structure. It also illustrated basic data structures like linked lists, BSTs, and the algorithms to work on them. There are many other data structures and algorithms that were not mentioned in the text. We recommend that the reader experiment with these concepts to get a clear understanding of pointers to structure.

In the next chapter, we will look into the concept of function pointers that help in making dynamic function calls.

CHAPTER 7

■ ■ ■

Function Pointers

Many times we come across situations where we have multiple functions that do specific jobs. Then, based on a particular situation, we need to call the proper function from that group. In this chapter, we will see how function pointers help us tackle those situations. Function pointers are variables that are used for pointing to the address of a function. With the help of a function pointer, we can invoke a function call. Interestingly, we can use the function pointers to implement late binding, where we don't know which particular function call to make beforehand.

Defining Function Pointers

As discussed in Chapter 1, the compiler compiles code/text into the actual program code that is stored in memory. This code contains functions and their logic. The function pointer variable will point to some location where the program has been stored in memory.

The function pointer variable definition is dependent on the function definition that needs to be pointed to by this variable. In its most generic form, it is defined as follows:

return type (< variable_name) (parameters list);*

Examples:

1. Function to be pointed: `int add( int x, int y);`

2. Function pointer to point to the above function: `int (*addfuncptr)( int x, int y);`

3. Function to be pointed to: `int* plus( int x, int y);`

4. Function pointer to point to the above function: `int* (*plusfuncptr)(int x, int y);`

Initializing Function Pointers

Initializing a function pointer variable can be done in two ways.

1. With the "address of" operator.

2. Via an implicit assignment.

The following source code illustrates two methods of initializing function pointers, which are mentioned above.

Source code. Fptr1.c

```
#include <malloc.h>
#include <stdio.h>
void mesg(int num )
{
    printf("Mesg no. %d\n", num);
}
```

```
int* add(int x, int y)
{
      int *z = (int*)malloc(sizeof(int));
      *z = 10;
      return z;
}
int main(int argc, char* argv[])
{
      int *t;
      void (*fpmsg)(int);        //function pointer variable to point to the function "mesg"
      int* (*addfptr)(int, int); //function pointer variable to point to the function "add"
      addfptr = &add;            //assignment using "address of" operator
      fpmsg = mesg;              //assignment using implicit method
      return 0;
}
```

Using Function Pointers

Function pointers are used to make function calls. Specifically, they help in choosing which function to call dynamically. Let's see how this is done using function pointers. Function pointers can invoke a function in the following ways.

Source code. Fptr2.c

```
#include <malloc.h>
#include <stdio.h>
void mesg(int num )
{
   printf("Mesg no. %d\n", num);
}
int main(int argc, char* argv[])
{
   int *t;
   void (*fpmsg1)(int);  //function pointer variable to point to the function "mesg"
   void (*fpmsg2)(int);  //function pointer variable to point to the function "mesg"
   fpmsg1 = mesg;
   fpmsg2 = mesg;
   fpmsg1( 10 );         // implicit method of invoking a function
   (*)fpmsg2( 20 );      // explicit way of invoking a function
   return 0;
}
fpmsg1( 10 );            // implicit method of invoking a function
(*)fpmsg2( 20 );         // explicit way of invoking a function
```

The two ways in which functions can be invoked are shown above.

Let's assume a situation where we want to switch between different search algorithm functions based upon a user's input. Also, we have the following algorithms implemented:

```
bool arraysearch(int n);
bool binarysearchtree(int n);
bool Linkedlistsearch(int n);
```

We can invoke these function calls dynamically with the help of a function pointer, as follows:

```
bool search( bool ((*funcptr)(int), int data)
{
    return (*funcptr)(data);
}
```

Above, we have created a function in which the first parameter or argument is a function pointer variable, and the second parameter or argument is the actual value that needs to be searched. Based upon the choice made by the user, we can pass the appropriate address of the functions listed above.

The following is the complete code illustration.

Source code. Fptr3.c

```
bool arraysearch(int data)
{
    //some code
    return true;
}

bool linkedlistsearch(int data)
{
    //some code
    return true;
}

bool binarysearch(int data)
{
    //some code
    return true;
}

bool search( bool (*funcptr)( int ), int data )
{
    return (*funcptr)(data);
}

int main(int argc, char* argv[])
{
    printf("Input Options\n");
    printf("1 arrsrch\n");
    printf("2 linkedlistsrch\n");
    printf("3 binarysrch\n");
    printf("4 exit\n");
    int choice = 0;
    int data;
    while(choice != 4)
    {
        printf("Input\n");
        scanf("%d", &choice);
        printf("Data to search\n");
        scanf("%d", &data);
```

```
   if(choice == 1)
   {
      search(arraysearch,data);          //invoking 1st function
   }
   else if(choice == 2)
   {
      search(linkedlistsearch, data); //invoking 2nd function
   }else if(choice == 3)
   {
      search(binarysearch, data);       //invoking  3rd function
   }
   else if(choice == 4)
         break;
  }
  return 0;
}
```

Assembly Details of Function Pointer Calls

In this section, we will look at a detailed view of the assembly code to show how the function call is made and compare it with the function call made with the help of the function pointer.

Invocation of Function Call Directly

Here is the assembler code that calls the function directly:

```
int add( int a, int b)
{
   int z = a + b;
   return z;
}

int main(int argc, char* argv[])
{
   int z = add(10,20);
   return 0;
}
```

Here is the assembler output where the function call is made directly:

```
      push    20                          ; 00000014H
      push    10                          ; 0000000aH
      call    ?add@@YAHHH@Z               ; add
      add     esp, 8
      mov     DWORD PTR _z$[ebp], eax
```

The assembly instruction call is executed to make a function call after pushing all the parameters to the stack. The highlighted assembly instruction above is an example of how the function is invoked.

Invocation of Function Call Indirectly with a Function Pointer

Function calls can be made via function pointers. This gives the ability to add amazing flexibility to your code, as you can change program behavior simply by changing pointer values. The following example illustrates the concept:

```
int add( int a, int b)
{
    int z = a + b;
    return z;
}

int main(int argc, char* argv[])
{
    int (*funcptr)(int x, int y) = add;
    funcptr(10,20);
    return 0;
}
```

Here is the assembler output showing how the function call is made through the function pointer:

```
mov      DWORD PTR _funcptr$[ebp], OFFSET ?add@@YAHHH@Z ; add
mov      esi, esp                                         push
20                              ; 00000014H
push     10                     ; 0000000aH
call     DWORD PTR _funcptr$[ebp]
add      esp, 8
cmp      esi, esp                                         call
__RTC_CheckEsp
```

In the assembly code above, the first highlighted assembly line "mov DWORD PTR _funcptr$[ebp], OFFSET ?add@@YAHHH@Z ; add" assigns the address of the function to the function pointer. The second highlighted assembly line " call DWORD PTR _funcptr$[ebp]" calls the function with the help of the function pointer.

Array of Function Pointers

An array of function pointers gives a way to switch between functions with the help of an array index.

Defining an Array of a Function Pointers

Defining an array of function pointers is a little bit cryptic in nature. It takes a generic form, which is explained below. We can use an array of function pointers for functions that have the same return types and the number of input parameters is equal and of the same type.

<return type of function being pointed> (*functionpointervariable [])(input parameters pointed by function being pointed to)

Example:

Assume we have four functions.

```
int add(int x, int y);
int sub(int x, int y);
int mul(int x, int y)
int div(int x, int y);
```

Now, we will define an array of function pointers to hold the addresses of the functions listed above and initialize them.

```
int (* opfunctptr [ ] ) ( int x, int y) = { add, sub, mul, div };
```

We can now invoke a function based on the array index as follows:

```
opfunctptr[ 0 ] ( 10 , 20 ); // This invokes the function add
```

Programmers need to be careful when using function pointer arrays because there is no bound check while accessing an array index. If the array is accessed out of an index, the control may land anywhere.

Returning Function Pointers from Function

Defining a function that returns a function pointer of a function is a tedious task and requires quite an effort. It can be done in two ways, easy and difficult.

Difficult Way

Let's make some assumptions to make the example easier to understand.

```
int add(int , int ); //function to be pointed to by the function pointer
//function returning the result after adding the values of two parameters
int (*addfuncptr)(int, int);
 //function pointer, capable of pointing to the above function "int add(int,int)"
```

Now comes the hard part; we intend to define a function that doesn't take any input but is capable of returning a function pointer as stated above, [int (*addfuncpt)(int, int)].
Preparing the skeleton of the function:

- **Write the name**: funcptrret

- **Specify input parameters for the function**: funcptrret(void)

- In this case it does not take any input parameter.

- **Add parenthesis and the value of operator**: (* funcptrret(void))

- **Add the details about the input parameter of the function pointer that needs to be returned**: In this case the [int (*addfuncptr)(int, int)] function pointer takes two input parameters (int, int).

  (* funcptrret(void))(int, int)

- **Add the details about the return parameter of the function pointer that needs to be returned**: In this case the [int (*addfuncptr)(int, int)] function pointer returns an int.

  int (* funcptrret(void))(int, int)

So, the desired function that returns the function pointer is declared as int (* funcptrret(void))(int, int).

Easy Way

Let's make similar assumptions to make the example easier to understand.

```
int add(int , int );  //function to be pointed  to by the function pointer
//function returning the result after adding the values of two parameters
int (*addfuncptr)(int, int);
 //function pointer, capable of pointing to the above function int add(int,int)
```

Preparing the skeleton of the function:

- **The typedef of the function pointer that needs to be returned:**

- *typedef int (* addfuncptr)(int p1, int p2);*

- **Write the name of the function and input parameter:** *funcptrret(void)*

- In this case, the function does not take any input.

- **Add the return parameter to the function:** *addfuncptr* funcptrret(void)

- We can use *typedef* above as the returning parameter.

So, the desired function that returns the function pointer is declared as ***addfuncptr funcptrret(void)***. The below source code illustrates how a function pointer can be returned from a function.

Source code. Fptr4.c

```
int myadd( int a, int b)
{
    int z = a + b;
    return z;
}
int mysub(int a, int b)
{
    int z = a - b;
    return z;
}
int mymul(int a, int b)
{
    int z = a*b;
    return z;
}
int mydiv(int a, int b)
{
    int z = a/b;
    return z;
}
//array of function pointers,
int (* opfunctptr [ ] ) ( int x, int y) = { myadd, mysub, mymul, mydiv };
typedef int (*calc)(int x, int y );
//function returning the function pointer of type int (*calc)(int x, int y )
```

```
calc retmathfunc(int index)
{
    return opfunctptr[index];
}
int main(int argc, char* argv[])
{
    int choice, p1, p2, res;
    int (*calculator)(int x, int y);
    printf("Type -1 to quit\n");
    printf("Type 0 - add, 1 - sub, 2 - mul, 3 - div\n");
    scanf("%d", &choice);
    while( choice != -1)
    {
        calculator = retmathfunc(choice); //returns function pointer
        printf("Param1\n");
        scanf("%d", &p1);
        printf("Param2\n");
        scanf("%d", &p2);
        res = calculator(p1, p2);         //calling function pointer
        printf("res = %d\n", res);
        printf("Type 0 - add, 1 - sub, 2 - mul, 3 - div\n");
        scanf("%d", &choice);
    }
    return 0;
}
```

Function Pointer Usage in the Linux Kernel

The most common use of function pointers in Linux can be found during device driver implementation. Linux maintains standard data structures for different types of hardware. There are standard functions (open, close, read, write, etc.) that need to be called for the specific hardware types. These function pointers are part of the data structure. Every device driver programmer implements these functions when writing drivers for specific devices. The programmer then populates the function pointer fields of the standard data structure and passes this standard data structure to the initialization routine. These steps are like registering function calls. When an instance of the data structure is loaded into memory and the function needs to be called for a specific device, the function pointers in the data structure can be used to invoke those functions for that device.

Below is an example of the netdevice.h header file taken from Linux kernel source code. It can be found at Linux/include/linux/netdevice.h. It contains all the important data structures and functions that are used by TCP/IP layer code.

Example of netdevice.h:

```
struct net_device_ops {
int        (*ndo_init)(struct net_device *dev);
void       (*ndo_uninit)(struct net_device *dev);
int        (*ndo_open)(struct net_device *dev);
int        (*ndo_stop)(struct net_device *dev);
netdev_tx_t        (*ndo_start_xmit) (struct sk_buff *skb, struct net_device *dev);
u16        (*ndo_select_queue)(struct net_device *dev, struct sk_buff *skb);
void       (*ndo_change_rx_flags)(struct net_device *dev,  int flags);
void       (*ndo_set_rx_mode)(struct net_device *dev);
int        (*ndo_set_mac_address)(struct net_device *dev,    void *addr);
```

```
int        (*ndo_validate_addr)(struct net_device *dev);
int        (*ndo_do_ioctl)(struct net_device *dev,   struct ifreq *ifr, int cmd);
int        (*ndo_set_config)(struct net_device *dev, struct ifmap *map);
int        (*ndo_change_mtu)(struct net_device *dev,   int new_mtu);
int        (*ndo_neigh_setup)(struct net_device *dev,  struct neigh_parms *);
void       (*ndo_tx_timeout) (struct net_device *dev);
```

The data structure above is defined to handle network devices. The member fields are function pointers that need to be implemented by the programmer writing the device driver for a specific device.

The following example shows how the structure above is filled with function pointers. This example is from the Linux source code for the driver r8169:

```
static const struct net_device_ops rtl_netdev_ops = {
        .ndo_open               = rtl_open,
        .ndo_stop               = rtl8169_close,
        .ndo_get_stats64        = rtl8169_get_stats64,
        .ndo_start_xmit         = rtl8169_start_xmit,
        .ndo_tx_timeout         = rtl8169_tx_timeout,
        .ndo_validate_addr      = eth_validate_addr,
        .ndo_change_mtu         = rtl8169_change_mtu,
        .ndo_fix_features       = rtl8169_fix_features,
        .ndo_set_features       = rtl8169_set_features,
        .ndo_set_mac_address    = rtl_set_mac_address,
        .ndo_do_ioctl           = rtl8169_ioctl,
        .ndo_set_rx_mode        = rtl_set_rx_mode,
#ifdef CONFIG_NET_POLL_CONTROLLER
        .ndo_poll_controller    = rtl8169_netpoll,
#endif
};
```

In the below function, devinitrtl_init_one() is a part of device driver code which is an initialization routine. In this function, registration of the structure net_device_ops is done.

```
static int __devinitrtl_init_one(struct pci_dev *pdev, const struct pci_device_id *ent)
{
const struct rtl_cfg_info *cfg = rtl_cfg_infos + ent->driver_data;
const unsigned int region = cfg->region;
struct rtl8169_private *tp;
struct mii_if_info *mii;
struct net_device *dev;
void __iomem *ioaddr;
int chipset, i;
int rc;
if (netif_msg_drv(&debug)) {
printk(KERN_INFO "%s Gigabit Ethernet driver %s loaded\n",
MODULENAME, RTL8169_VERSION);
}
dev = alloc_etherdev(sizeof (*tp));
if (!dev) {
rc = -ENOMEM;
goto out;
}
```

```
SET_NETDEV_DEV(dev, &pdev->dev);
dev->netdev_ops = &rtl_netdev_ops;
tp = netdev_priv(dev);
tp->dev = dev;
tp->pci_dev = pdev;
tp->msg_enable = netif_msg_init(debug.msg_enable, R8169_MSG_DEFAULT);
```

The italicized text above shows the portion of code where the data structure and eventually the function pointers are getting registered and can be used later as callback functions.

Summary of Cryptic Function Pointer Declarations

Many cryptic function pointer declarations are illustrated below. A function can return different data types and it can also return pointers of a different data type. For functions of different types, there will be function pointers that can be used to point them. For each point below, it first takes an example of a function and also declares its corresponding function pointer. In some points the declarations are made more complex.

- Function: `int add(int x, int y);`

- Function ptr: `int (*addfptr)(int x, int y);`

- Function: `int* add(int x, int y);`

- Function ptr: `int* (*addfptr)(int x, int y);`

- Function: `int add(int x, int y);`

- Function ptr: `int (*addfptr)(int x, int y);`

- Function whose input parameter is a function pointer as above and return type is void:
  `void callfunc(int (*addfptr)(int x, int y));`

- Function: `int add(int x, int y);`

- Function ptr: `int (*addfptr)(int x, int y);`

- Pointer to a function pointer to a function returning int: `int (*(*addfptr))(int x, int y);`

- Function: `int add(int x, int y);`

- Function ptr: `int (*addfptr)(int x, int y);`

- Function whose input parameter is void and return type is function pointer:

- `int (*retfuncptr(void)(int x, int y );`

- Function: `int* add(int x, int y);`

- function ptr: `int* (*addfptr)(int x, int y);`

- function whose input parameter is void and return type is function pointer:

- `int* (*retfuncptr(void)(int x, int y);`

Summary

In this chapter we covered one of the most interesting aspects of programming. Dynamic invocation of function calls helps in situations when we need to decide which function needs to be called during runtime. In other words, think of function pointers as the hooks that will help in making the required function calls.

CHAPTER 8

■ ■ ■

Pointers to File I/O

We all use computer file systems and interact directly or indirectly with them as programmers or ordinary system users. All our persistent data and files are kept in secondary memory. The file system manages data and provides interfaces to retrieve and store data in secondary memory. By *secondary memory* is meant all the external memory drives such as HDD and USB drive which do not include RAM. The file system also provides an interface for the operating system to manage the space in secondary memory.

This chapter explores the I/O aspects of file pointers. It discusses in detail how the C library APIs are used to manipulate data with the help of file pointers. It also supplies information about secondary memory and file systems.

The Physical Layout of Secondary Memory

Let's take a look at the structural details of secondary memory. Typically, secondary memory is a stack of magnetic discs that are capable of storing information on both of the faces. These discs are called *platters* and each face is called a *surface*. These platters are stacked on a spindle that is rotated by a motor.

Each surface of a platter is further divided into concentric rings called *tracks*. The *cylinder value is* the number of tracks on each side of a platter. In turn, these tracks are further grouped into *sectors*. A sector is the smallest portion of the architecture that actually stores data.

Reading the data from these media is accomplished with the help of a *disk head* that is provided for each surface. This disk head is attached with the help of an arm that moves while reading different sectors.

Surface View

Figure 8-1 shows the top view of a surface on which data is stored in each sector. Each sector is typically able to store 512 bytes.

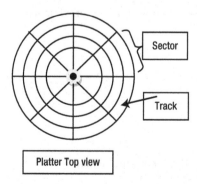

Figure 8-1. *Platter top view*

For the operating system, the basic unit of data transfers for I/O is the *block*, which is a group of sectors. The grouping can comprise of 2, 4, 8, or more sectors per block. Figure 8-2 illustrates the head, which is used to read the desired tracks from a particular sector.

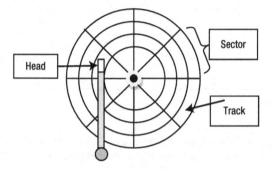

Figure 8-2. *The head of a disc*

Interfacing HDD with CPU

How does a CPU interact with a disk drive? The *disk controller* is the entity that takes care of the communication of data and command between a CPU and a disk drive.

You have heard the names of many controllers, such as SATA controller for SATA disks, SCSI, IDE, and so on. Disk controllers perform the following tasks:

- Receiving commands from the CPU (read, write, etc.)

- Implementing drive interface logic to control the arm motion

- Using read/write logic to serialize parallel data

Disk Addressing Schemes

A *disk addressing scheme* is a method to identify the sectors on a disk by their positions in a track. There are two schemes by which the addressing of sectors takes place: CHS addressing and LBA addressing.

CHS Addressing

In earlier days, the parameters used for addressing were C, H, and S (which represent the total number of cylinders, heads, and sectors within the track). The ranges of these parameters were as follows:

- **C:** The cylinder numbers range between 0 to C-1.

- **H:** 0 to H-1.

- **S:** 1- S.

LBA Addressing

LBA addressing uses only one parameter. These parameters are sector numbers 0, 1, 2, 3, etc. This method is used with SCSI and IDE disk drives for location purposes for the cylinders, heads, and sectors.

Introduction to File System Architecture

This section provides an overview of file system architecture. It does not discuss any specific file system, but the examples and explanations touch on the details from existing file systems that will help in elaborating the concept. A high-level schematization of file system architecture is shown in Figure 8-3.

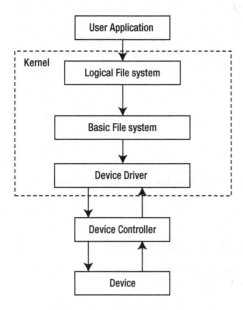

Figure 8-3. *File system architecture*

Logical File System

A *logical file system* provides a way or abstraction for viewing the files. It generally has two main logical entities—file and directory—and a hierarchical structure.

A logical file system manages an inode structure. *Inode* is an on-disk structure that is used to manage all the files on the disk. Inode consists of all the following information for managing a file:

- Type (Directory/File)

- Protection levels

- Block information pertaining to that file

- Time stamp for creation/modification of file, etc.

- Directory structure (per file system) organizes the files.

- Volume control block (per volume) contains superblock (UFS) and the master file table (NTFS).

- Boot control block (per volume), called boot block (UFS)

- I/O control: The programs which do the actual data transfer are part of I/O control. Device drivers and special interrupt service routines which communicate with devices are those programs.

The Basic File System

The *basic file system* interacts with device drivers and issues generic low-level commands to it. This layer also deals with the management of blocks on the disk.

What Is Required to Make a File System?

The most important thing that is required to keep account of data and the places where it resides is the data structures. Data structures play a very important role in creating and maintaining a file system. In the context of the file system, data structures are categorized in two ways.

- On-disk data structures

- In-memory data structures

On-Disk Data Structures

A preceding section defined the data structure, inode. We need to make this data structure persistent since it contains all the information about the data stored in the file system. The inode is stored in a block that is called an inode table. A block is a logical representation of sectors and cylinders.

The other data structures that are stored on the disk are as follows:

- **Boot control block**: The information kept here is used to boot the OS from a partition.

- **Partition control block**: This is also called a *superblock*. This block contains information about the free blocks, details of the partition where blocks are mapped, and so forth.

In-Memory Data Structures

Some readers might be aware of the details surrounding this process and the information attached to in-memory data structures. For each process in memory, the operating system has a file table data structure associated with it. This helps in keeping track of the number of files opened by the process. The following are data structures that are loaded in memory while interacting with the file system:

- The file table associated with each process

- The directory structure

- A partition table

Accessing Files

C provides various functions for manipulating files residing on the secondary disc. A buffer is involved when interacting with a file, and the operating system uses this buffer to improve the efficiency of I/O. C provides a data structure FILE to use as an object to interact with an actual file in order to manipulate it and its data in memory.

For most of the function calls such as open, close, delete, etc., a pointer of type FILE is used. The FILE data structure is defined in the C header file called *stdio.h*.

FILE Data Structure

As mentioned above, the FILE data structure is defined in the *stdio.h* header file. It contains file stream information. It also contains information about the file position and buffer. In the *stdio.h* file, special kinds of file streams are defined that are used to denote some specialized devices.

- STDIN: This value is used to denote an input stream.

- STDOUT: This value is used to denote an output stream.

- STDERROR: This stream is used to denote any stand error.

This operation is very similar to strings, where the null character '\0' is used to denote the end of string. Here, however, we have an EOF value associated with a file to denote that there is an end of data. This value is a negative integer constant.

First Task

To manipulate the file or the data within it, we must open it. We cannot do anything without opening a file. Let's take a look at the first call of opening a file.

```
FILE* fopen(char* filename, char* mode);
```

This function takes the path of the file name to be worked upon as a first input parameter; the second parameter is the mode (such as r, w, or a) in which the file needs to be opened. The following explains the three mode options:

- **Read mode (r)**: Opens the file in read mode. If the file does not exist, the function call returns null.

- **Write mode (w)**: Opens the file in write mode. If the file does not exist, the function call creates a new file. If the file exists, then the old content of the file is overwritten.

- **Append mode (a)**: Opens the file in append mode. If the file exists, the new content is written after the end of the file. If the file does not exist, then a new file is created.

(Other modes—such as r+, w+, a+—are not discussed here.)

This function returns a pointer of type FILE structure when the opening of the file is successful. The following code illustrates the usage of *fopen()* function call.

Source code. FileProg1.c

```
#include <stdio.h>
int main(int argc, char* argv[])
{
    FILE* fp = NULL;
    fp = fopen("c:\\test.txt","w");
    if(fp == NULL)
    {
        printf("File opening error\n");
    }
```

```
        else
        {
            printf("File opening success\n");
        }
        return 0;
}
```

The program above illustrates how a file is opened in write mode using the *fopen* call and then the FILE pointer needs to be checked against NULL to make sure that the file opening operation was successful before doing anything with the file and its data.

Second Task

For a process, a file is a resource. If a process opens a file, it needs to be released after the operation/manipulation is over. For releasing this resource, we use another function call that is the counterpart of the *fopen()* function call. The function call that is used to close an opened file is *fclose()*.

```
int fclose ( FILE * fptr )
```

This function takes a file pointer as an input parameter and returns 0 on success or EOF on failure. The following source code illustrates the usage of the *fclose()* function call.

Source code. FileProg2.c

```
#include <stdio.h>
int main(int argc, char* argv[])
{
    FILE* fp = NULL;
    int res;
    fp = fopen("c:\\test.txt","w");
    if(fp == NULL)
    {
        printf("File opening error\n");
    }
    else
    {
        printf("File opening success\n");
    }
    res = fclose(fp);
    if(res == 0)
    {
        printf("File closed\n");
    }
    else
    {
        printf("Unable to close file\n");
    }
    return 0;
}
```

After the function is called, the result is compared to check the success and failure in the consecutive if and else statements. Before closing the file, the function call makes sure that it flushes all the data that is in memory and is written to the disk. Otherwise, some data may get lost.

Reading from a File

For reading the content/data from a file, C has provided many functions that can be used according to the programmer's needs. The following are a few of the methods, which the next sections look at in detail:

- Reading a single character at a time from a file

- Reading strings from a file

- Reading block of data from a file

- Formatted reading from a file

Let's see these functions in detail.

Reading a Single Character

To read a character from a file, C has provided the following function:

```
int fgetc(FILE *fptr);
```

When this function is called, the file pointer returns the character that it is pointing to and then it advances the file pointer to the next character. This function call returns an integer value of the character that was read from the file buffer.

Assuming that we have a test file (*test.txt*) to read, and the contents of the file are

abcde

fghij

klmno

pqrst

uvwxyz

Let's see how this function call helps in reading a file.

Source code. FileProg3.c

```
#include <stdio.h>
int main(int argc, char* argv[])
{
    FILE* fp = NULL;
    int res;
    int data;
    fp = fopen("c:\\test.txt","w");
    if(fp == NULL)
    {
        printf("File opening error\n");
    }
```

```
        else
        {
            printf("File opening success\n");
        }
        while((data = fgetc(fp)) != EOF)
        {
            if ( data != 10) //checking for new line
                printf("%d %c ,", data, (char)data);
            else
            {
                printf{"\n");
            }
        }
        res = fclose(fp);
        if(res == 0)
        {
            printf("File closed\n");
        }
        else
        {
            printf("Unable to close file\n");
        }
        return 0;
}
```

Output:

```
File opening success
1, 2, 3, 4, 5,
6, 7, 8, 9, 10,
11, 12, 13, 14, 15,
16, 17, 18, 19, 20,
21, 22, 23, 24, 25,
```

This program illustrates the use of the *fgetc()* function call. Every time the function is called, the returned value is checked against the EOF to know whether we have reached the end of file. Thus, in the *while* loop we can iterate and read each character one at a time.

Reading Strings from a File

We can use the *fgets()* function to read a set of bytes. The details of using the function call for reading the strings are as follows:

```
char * fgets ( char * str, int length, FILE * fptr )
```

This function takes a character pointer as an input that is filled by the characters read from the buffer; a second input parameter is the length of the characters that needs to be read. The number of characters that needs to be read is always **length – 1** and the last parameter is the file pointer variable obtained after calling the *fopen()* function.

Upon opening success, this function returns a pointer to the first input parameter and returns NULL on failure. Upon reading the characters from the input string, this function also appends a null terminating character '\0' at the end of the string.

Source code. FileProg4.c

```c
#include <malloc.h>
#define BUFFER 4
int main(int argc, char * argv[])
{
    FILE* fp;
    int res;
    char*str = NULL;
    unsigned char chr;
    int fpos;
    fp = fopen("c:\\test.txt","r");
    if(fp == NULL)
    {
        printf("File opening error\n");
    }
    else
    {
        printf("File opening success\n");
    }
    str = (char*)malloc(sizeof(char)*BUFFER);
    fpos = ftell(fp);
    printf("File pointer pos before reading = %d\n", fpos);
    if(fgets(str, BUFFER, fp))
    {
        printf("%s \n",str);
    }
    else
    {
        printf("Line reading failure\n");
    }
    fpos = ftell(fp);
    printf("File pointer pos after reading = %d\n", fpos);
    res = fclose(fp);
    if(res == 0)
    {
        printf("File closed\n");
    }
    else
    {
        printf("Unable to close file\n");
    }
    return 0;
}
```

Output:

```
File opening success
File pointer pos before reading = 0
abc
File pointer pos after reading = 3
File closed
```

131

In this program, the function call *ftell()* is used to find the current position of the file pointer before and after calling the *fgets()* function. We can see from the output that after reading three characters from the buffer, the file position indicator is pointing to a fourth character.

Reading Blocks from File

The *fread()* function can be used for reading the data in blocks from a file. The details of the function call are as follows:

```
size_t fread(void *ptr, size_t size, size_t n, FILE * fptr);
```

The first parameter, *void* ptr*, is the input parameter of type void pointer to which the data read from buffer will be copied. The second parameter, *size_t size*, is the input parameter that specifies the size of each data block. The third parameter, *size_t n*, specifies the number of bytes to be read. The fourth parameter is *FILE* fptr*. The return parameter of the function returns the number of data read when successful. There is a difference in the value of the return parameter and the third input parameter when there is an error while reading or the file pointer indicator has reached the EOF.

The following source code illustrates the usage of *fread()* function call, which enables the program to read the data in blocks from a file.

Source code. FileProg5.c

```c
#include <stdio.h>
#include <malloc.h>
#define BUFFER 5
int main(int argc, char* argv[])
{
    FILE* fp;
    int res;
    char*str = NULL;
    fp = fopen("c:\\test.txt","r");
    if(fp == NULL)
    {
        printf("File opening error\n");
    }
    else
    {
        printf("File opening success\n");
    }
    str = (char*)malloc(sizeof(char)*BUFFER);
    res = fread(str, sizeof(char), BUFFER-1, fp);
    str[4] = '\0';
    if(res)
    {
        printf("%s \n",str);
    }
    else
    {
        printf("Line reading failure\n");
    }
```

```
    res = fclose(fp);
    if(res == 0)
    {
        printf("File closed\n");
    }
    else
    {
        printf("Unable to close file\n");
    }
    return 0;
}
```

In this code, we are trying to read characters. This function call reads the block of characters and stores them in the assigned memory area. Note that this function call does not append terminating null characters at the end; it is the responsibility of the programmer to do so if this function call is used to read the characters.

Formatted Reading from File

There are situations when data in the file is written in a particular format. For example, in some columns, when each column is separated with a space and each column contains data in some context, such as:

```
Index First_name Country
```

To read this kind of formatted data in some variable, we can use the following function call:

```
int fscanf ( FILE * stream, const char * format, … )
```

The first parameter is the file pointer. The second parameter specifies the format. The return parameter is an integer that returns the number of data that is matched to the pattern or it can return 0 if there is no match and this condition is true in case of success. In case of failure, it returns EOF.

The following source code illustrates the usage of the *fscanf()* function call.

Source code. FileProg6.c

```
#include<stdio.h>
#include<malloc.h>
int main(int argc, char* argv[])
{
    FILE* fp;
    int res;
    int index;
    char* name = NULL;
    char* country = NULL;
    fp = fopen("c:\\test.txt","r");
    if(fp == NULL)
    {
        printf("File opening error\n");
    }
    else
    {
        printf("File opening success\n");
    }
```

```
   name = (char*)malloc(sizeof(char)*BUFFER);
   country = (char*)malloc(sizeof(char)*BUFFER);
   while (!feof(fp))
   {
       fscanf(fp, "%d %s %s", &index, name, country);
       printf("%d %s %s\n", index, name, country);
   }
   res = fclose(fp);
   if(res == 0)
   {
       printf("File closed\n");
   }
   else
   {
       printf("Unable to close file\n");
   }
   return 0;
}
```

Writing to a File

In the previous section, we saw many function calls that enable us to read the input stream. C has also provided their counterparts to write the content/data into a file. The following are a few of the methods, which the next sections look at in detail:

- Writing a single character at a time to the file

- Writing strings to the file

- Writing a block of data to the file

Let's look at these functions in detail.

Writing a Single Character to a File

To write any data byte by byte to a file, we can use the following function call:

```
int fputc ( int data, FILE * fptr );
```

The first parameter is the input data that needs to be written to the file. The second parameter is the file pointer that is the file handle. The third parameter is the returning parameter that outputs the character that is returned on success. In case of failure, it returns EOF.

The following source code illustrates the usage of *fputc()* function call, which helps in writing a single character to a file.

Source code. FileProg7.c

```
#include<stdio.h>
#include<malloc.h>
int main(int argc, char* argv[])
{
    FILE* fp;
    int res;
```

```
    int index;
    char* namefmt = "First Middle Last";
    fp = fopen("c:\\test.txt","w");
    if(fp == NULL)
    {
        printf("File opening error\n");
        return 0;
    }
    else
    {
        printf("File opening success\n");
    }
    for( index = 0; index <= strlen(namefmt); index++)
    {
        fputc(namefmt[index], fp);
    }
    res = fclose(fp);
    if(res == 0)
    {
        printf("File closed\n");
    }
    else
    {
        printf("Unable to close file\n");
    }
    return 0;
}
```

Here, we iterate over each index of the array and *fputc* is called. In addition, the file has been opened in w mode, which will erase the previous content of the file if there was any.

Writing a String onto the File

Let's see the function call that will help in writing a set of bytes into the file at a time.

```
int fputs ( const char * str, FILE * fptr )
```

The first input parameter is the character string that we want to write to the file. The second input parameter is the file pointer. The third parameter is the output that returns a non-negative value in case of success and an end of file in case of EOF.

The following source code illustrates the usage of *fputs()* function call. It explains how a string can be written to a file.

Source code. FileProg8.c

```
#include<stdio.h>
#include<malloc.h>
int main(int argc, char* argv[])
{
    FILE* fp;
    int res;
```

```
    int index;
    char* namefmt = "First Middle Last";
    fp = fopen("c:\\test.txt","w");
    if(fp == NULL)
    {
        printf("File opening error\n");
        return 0;
    }
    else
    {
        printf("File opening success\n");
    }
    fputs(namefmt, fp);
    res = fclose(fp);
    if(res == 0)
    {
        printf("File closed\n");
    }
    else
    {
        printf("Unable to close file\n");
    }
    return 0;
}
```

Again, in the code above, the file is being opened in write mode and the *fputs()* function is called.

Writing a Block of Data to a File

The *fwrite()* function is the counterpart of the *fread()* function. This function can be used to write a block of data to the file.

```
size_t fwrite(const void *ptr, size_t size, size_t n, FILE *fptr);
```

The first parameter is the pointer to the data memory that needs to be written to the file. The second parameter is the size of each datum. The third parameter is the number of data to be written. The fourth parameter is the file pointer. The fifth output parameter is the number of data which is written successfully. In case of success, the value of fifth parameter is equal to the value of third parameter. In case of failure, the value of fifth parameter is less than the value of third parameter.

The following source code illustrates the usage of writing a block of data to a file with the help of *fwrite()* function call.

Source code. FileProg9.c

```
#include<stdio.h>
int main(int argc, char* argv[])
{
    FILE* fp;
    int res;
    int index;
    int numofdatatowrite;
```

```
    char* namefmt = "First Middle Last";
    fp = fopen("c:\\test.txt","w");
    if(fp == NULL)
    {
        printf("File opening error\n");
        return 0;
    }
    else
    {
        printf("File opening success\n");
    }
    numofdatatowrite = 5;
    if(numofdatatowrite == fwrite(namefmt, sizeof(char), numofdatatowrite, fp))
    {
        printf("Success in writing data\n");
    }
    else
        printf("Unsuccess in writing data\n");
    res = fclose(fp);
    if(res == 0)
    {
        printf("File closed\n");
    }
    else
    {
        printf("Unable to close file\n");
    }
    return 0;
}
```

The program above illustrates how the data from a character pointer is written to the file using the *fwrite* function call.

Accessing Disk at Random Locations

There are situations when a programmer wants to read data from random locations (beginning of file, end of file, somewhere in between). There are a couple of functions provided by C that can be used to access the file's locations randomly.

Seeking the File Indicator

The *fseek()* function call is used for maneuvering the file pointer to different locations.

```
int fseek(FILE *fptr, long off, int whence);
```

The first parameter is the file pointer of the file on which we are operating. The second parameter is the offset where we need to position the file indicator next, and this position is relative to the third parameter. The third parameter dictates the second parameter's meaning based upon its value:

- SEEK_SET: Beginning of the file; the offset is relative to the beginning of the file.

- SEEK_CUR: Current position indicator; the offset is relative to the current position of the file indicator.

- SEEK_END: End of file; offset is relative to the end of file.

The fourth output return parameter returns zero when *fseek()* is successful or a non-zero value when it's not. The following source code illustrates the usage of *fseek()* function call.

Source code. FileProg10.c

```c
#include<stdio.h>
#include<malloc.h>
int main(int argc, char* argv[])
{
    FILE* fp;
    int res;
    int index;
    char* datafromfile = (char*)malloc(sizeof(char)*6);
    fp = fopen("c:\\test.txt","w");
    if(fp == NULL)
    {
        printf("File opening error\n");
        return 0;
    }
    else
    {
        printf("File opening success\n");
    }
    fputs("HELLO NAV", fp);
    fclose(fp);
    fp = fopen("c:\\test.txt","r");
    //Read the current content
    fgets(datafromfile, 10, fp);
    printf("Current content of file %s\n", datafromfile);
    rewind(fp);      //resetting the file pointer
    fseek(fp, 6, SEEK_SET);//seeks file pointer to offset value 6 from beginning of file
    memset(datafromfile, 0, sizeof(char));
    fgets(datafromfile, 6, fp);
    printf("Content of data %s\n", datafromfile);
    fseek(fp, 0L, SEEK_SET); //seeks file pointer to offset value 0 from beginning of file
    memset(datafromfile, 0, sizeof(char));
    fgets(datafromfile, 6, fp);
    printf("Content of data %s\n", datafromfile);
    fclose(fp);
    return 0;
}
```

Output:

```
File opening success
Current content of file HELLO NAV
Content of data NAV
Content of data HELLO
```

The *fseek()* function has set the file pointer to offset 6 and reads the data from that position. Then *fseek()* sets the file pointer to the offset 0 and reads the data from that position.

Miscellaneous Functions

So far you have seen how to use functions to read and write to a file. You also saw how these functions manipulate the file pointer. You will now see some miscellaneous functions that also help in manipulating a function pointer.

Knowing the Size of File

First, let's look at a function called *ftell()*:

```
long int ftell ( FILE * fptr );
```

This function takes the file pointer as an input parameter and returns the current position of the file pointer's location upon success and returns -1 on failure. The following source code illustrates the usage of the *ftell()* function call. The first *ftell()* function calls returns the position of the file pointer. Next, the *fseek()* function call is made, which moves the file pointer ahead. Then the *ftell()* function call is made again. This second *ftell()* function call returns the current position of the file pointer.

Source code. FileProg11.c

```
int main(int argc, char* argv[])
{
        FILE* fp;
        int fileoffset = 0;
        fp = fopen("c:\\test.txt","w");
        if(fp == NULL)
        {
                printf("File opening error\n");
                return 0;
        }
        else
        {
                printf("File opening success\n");
        }
        fputs("HELLO NAV", fp);
        fclose(fp);
        fp = fopen("c:\\test.txt","r");
        fileoffset = ftell(fp);
        printf("File offset at default position %d\n", fileoffset);
        fseek(fp, 6, SEEK_SET);
        fileoffset = ftell(fp);
        printf("File offset after seeking %d\n", fileoffset);
```

```
        fclose(fp);
        return 0;
}
```

Output:

```
File opening success
File offset at default position 0
File offset after seeking 6
```

This code illustrates the use of the *ftell()* function to get the current position of the file offset.

To determine the size of a file, we will use the *fseek()* and *ftell()* functions in the following source code.

Source code. FileProg12.c

```
int main(int argc, char* argv[])
{
        FILE* fp;
            int fileoffset=0;           fp = fopen("c:\\test.txt","w");
        if(fp == NULL)
        {
                printf("File opening error\n");
                return 0;
        }
        else
        {
                printf("File opening success\n");
        }
        fputs("HELLO NAV", fp);
        fclose(fp);
        fp = fopen("c:\\test.txt","r");
        fseek(fp, 0, SEEK_END);
        fileoffset = ftell(fp);
        printf("Size of file in bytes %d\n", fileoffset);
        fclose(fp);
        return 0;
}
```

Output:

```
File opening success
Size of file in bytes 9
```

In this code, the *fseek()* call is made using the SEEK_END parameter that places the file offset to the end of the file buffer. Since, in this case the total count for the characters is 9, so the file offset is pointing to the last character. Then, with the help of the *ftell()* function we get the location of the file offset.

Another Way of Resetting the Position of File

The *fseek()* function call can be used to bring the position of the file offset back to the beginning of the file buffer, but there is another function call that does the same.

```
void rewind ( FILE * fptr );
```

This function call takes a file pointer as an input parameter that upon success sets the position of the file offset to the beginning of file buffer. The following source code illustrates the usage of the rewind function call. In it, after the *fgets()* function call is made, the file pointer gets incremented. At this point, the *rewind()* call resets the file handle and enables the program to read the file data from the beginning of the file buffer.

Source code. FileProg13.c

```
int main(int argc, char* argv[])
{
        FILE* fp;
        int fileoffset = 0;
        char* data = (char*)malloc(sizeof(char)*11);
        int val;
        fp = fopen("c:\\test.txt","r");
        if(fp == NULL)
        {
                printf("File opening error\n");
                return 0;
        }
        else
        {
                printf("File opening success\n");
        }
        if(fgets(data, 10, fp))
        {
                printf("%s \n",data);
        }
        else
        {
                printf("Line reading failure\n");
        }
        rewind(fp); //resetting the file offset to the beginning of file
        while((val = fgetc(fp)) != EOF)
        {
                if(val != 10) //checking for new line
                {
                        printf("%c",(char)val);
                }
                else
                {
                        printf("\n");
                }
        }
        fclose(fp);
        return 0;
}
```

Summary

This chapter covered secondary memory structure and file system architecture. It also covered various calls for reading and writing data to a file. One of the most important things to remember while updating the data in a file is to use the *fclose()* function call. The first reason to do so is to release the resource (file) via this call. The second reason is that, because the file is buffered into memory, the OS won't write the data until that memory buffer is full or the *fclose()* function is called. This chapter did not cover various other file management-related function calls, such as *freopen()*, *tmpfile()*, *fflush()*, and *ungetc()*, which are not strictly relevant to the scope of this work but which I encourage the reader to explore independently.

Index

A

Arithmetic operations, 43. *See also* Single
    dimension arrays
  addition
    assembler's output, 48
    compiler performs, 48
    integer variable, 46
    + operator, 46
    pointer variable, 47
  consecutively (memory blocks), 46
  operators, 46
  particular index, 46
  subtraction (-)
    comparing two pointer variables, 50
    conversion, 49
    integer location, 49
    pointer variable, 48–49
    subtracting two pointer variables, 49
Array(s). *See* Single dimension arrays
Array of pointers, 54
Array of strings
  declaration
    array notation, 65–67
    factors, 64
    freeing memory (steps), 69
    freestring() method, 67
    memory layout, 65
    pointer-to-pointer, 67–68
    storing data, 64–65
  memory layout, 64

B

Binary search tree (BST)
  creation, 110
  iterate over nodes, 111
  value storing nodes, 109
Boot control block, 126

C

Cache memory, 5
Consecutive memory locations, 92
Constants, 36
  constant pointer variable, 36
  pointer-constant variable, 37
  pointer-variable, 38
Cryptic function pointer
    declarations, 122

D

2D array
  1D context
    access the value
     (location/indexes), 72
    array arithmetic, 72
    variable name, 72
  2D context
    access 2D indices, 77–78
    arithmetic operation, 74
    location value, 75–77
    variable name, 73
3D array layout
  basics, 80
  expressions
    arithmetic operation, 82–87
    individual element, 87–88
    variable name, 81
  stack element, 79
Data structures and algorithms
  addatend() function, 109
  binary search tree
    creation, 110
    value storing nodes, 109
  iterate over nodes, 111
  linked list, 108
Dynamic array, 52

143

Get the eBook for only $10!

Now you can take the weightless companion with you anywhere, anytime. Your purchase of this book entitles you to 3 electronic versions for only $10.

This Apress title will prove so indispensible that you'll want to carry it with you everywhere, which is why we are offering the eBook in 3 formats for only $10 if you have already purchased the print book.

Convenient and fully searchable, the PDF version enables you to easily find and copy code—or perform examples by quickly toggling between instructions and applications. The MOBI format is ideal for your Kindle, while the ePUB can be utilized on a variety of mobile devices.

Go to www.apress.com/promo/tendollars to purchase your companion eBook.

Apress®

THE EXPERT'S VOICE™